JOHNSON
AND
ENGLISH POETRY BEFORE 1660

PRINCETON STUDIES IN ENGLISH
EDITED BY G. H. GEROULD
13

JOHNSON

AND

ENGLISH POETRY BEFORE 1660

BY

W. B. C. WATKINS

Instructor in English, Princeton University

NEW YORK
GORDIAN PRESS, INC.
1965

Originally Published 1936
Reprinted 1965

PREFACE

THE scope of this subject (spanning some eight centuries in the brain of a great man) precludes exhaustive treatment; though it would be interesting to carry the investigation further, it is questionable whether it would be really profitable. The material gathered here from the first and the revised editions of the *Dictionary,* his notes on Shakespeare, and his other works is sufficient to indicate clearly the nature and extent of Johnson's knowledge of English poetry before 1660.

The occasional introduction of prose statistics in a study concerned ostensibly only with poetry requires explanation. The most conspicuous instance is in the discussion of the Old and Middle English periods, for the sake of completeness. Otherwise, prose writers are mentioned, sparingly, for supplementary information.

Apart from a certain amount of definite proof, the purpose of the Appendix is to give a few concrete examples of Johnson's method and sources in compiling the *Dictionary.* It illustrates his occasional haphazard quotation (from Camden, notes of other editors on Shakespeare, etc.), his avoidance, whether intentional or careless, of such easy helps as the *Muses Library* and the *British Muse,* and his fairly accurate transcription of text. Also, it serves as an indication of the type of edition he used for quotation—sometimes eighteenth century, sometimes sixteenth or seventeenth. Johnson probably took whichever was most convenient, but we should remember that he not only knew but 'loved the old black letter books.'

I owe much to Professor D. Nichol Smith for increasing my interest in the eighteenth century; his stimulus as a teacher I shall always remember. I am very grateful to several of my colleagues: Professors G. H. Gerould, A. E. Hinds, C. G. Osgood, R. K. Root, and D. A. Stauffer. This study would not have been published—at least for some time—except for the Council of the Humanities at Princeton. I wish to thank them for their kindness, and especially the Secretary, Professor A. M. Friend.

W. B. C. WATKINS

CONTENTS

	PAGE
PREFACE	V
INTRODUCTION	I
EIGHTEENTH CENTURY LIBRARIES AND JOHNSON'S MANNER OF READING	16
JOHNSON AND NORTHERN LEARNING (871-1380)	28
CHAUCER TO SPENSER (1380-1579)	38
SPENSER TO THE RESTORATION (1579-1660)	58

APPENDIX—Sources Used for the *Dictionary*

I	Anglo-Saxon	85
II	Ballads	87
III	Barclay	90
IV	Camden	91
V	Chaucer	92
VI	Cooper (*Muses Library*)	94
VII	Davies	95
VIII	Donne	96
IX	Drayton	99
X	Elizabethan Drama	101
XI	Elizabethan Non-Dramatic Poetry	103
XII	Gower	106
XIII	Hayward (*British Muse*)	106
XIV	Lydgate	107
XV	Mandeville	108
XVI	Robert of Gloucester	108
XVII	Skelton	108
XVIII	Tottel's *Miscellany*	109
XIX	Wycliff	110

SOURCES	III
INDEX	115

'. . . his idea of poetry was magnificent indeed, and very fully was he persuaded of its superiority over every other talent bestowed by heaven on man. His chapter upon that particular subject in his Rasselas, is really written from the fulness of his heart.'

—*Mrs. Piozzi*

'Yet let not each gay Turn thy rapture move;
For fools admire, but men of sense approve.'

—*Pope*

INTRODUCTION

JOHNSON'S *Dictionary* embodies a personality; this differentiates it from all others. We can trace his progress so closely at times that we almost surprise him among a jumble of books, turning with an outflung arm to his assistants, or handing over with a contemptuous shrug his copy of the 1736 edition of Skelton, after marking in black lead pencil the passage he has chosen. Not the Preface alone, but the choice of illustrative quotations, the very definitions of words reflect his character and personal tastes. We may read his reminiscences of the lexicographer's trials in the *Rambler,* his letters pleading with friends for the loan of more books or explaining to Mr. Millar his difficulties with his amanuenses and get an extraordinarily clear picture of him at work on his vast undertaking, struggling to overcome his discouragements and his constitutional inertia; but we can learn all that from the *Dictionary* itelf. The study of his methods, of the editions he used for quotation, and particularly of his mistakes brings him startlingly close.

If Johnson's personality is everywhere evident in so barren a task as a dictionary, we can more readily understand its predominance in all his work and why a knowledge of his personality is essential before we judge anything he ever said or wrote. This is particularly true of his literary criticism. A creative mind has a natural tendency to impress its own image upon any metal, alloy or pure; and in this instance the personal element is emphasized by a peculiar train of circumstance.

Consider how many of Johnson's critical dicta were uttered in the course of ordinary conversation, taken down and preserved by Boswell, Fanny Burney, Mrs. Thrale, and others, or were dashed off in haste for a *Rambler* and sent along to the printer without so much as a rereading. Johnson over a period of years trained himself untiringly to think and speak and write with care and accuracy, so revision with him in a sense was not necessary; but, thanks to the zeal of his friends, no critic in English literature has had to stand so much responsibility for remarks made frequently in a burst of irritation, stung perhaps by one of Boswell's gadfly queries; no other critic has had admitted to the general body of his criticism such a large element of chance comment. Too many writers on Johnson have underestimated this fact,[1] have sometimes carelessly, sometimes intentionally taken advantage of casual or isolated comments to inveigh against the prejudice, the stubborn stupidity of the Great Bear.

I am not contending that all of Johnson's prejudices should be explained away or attributed to indigestion; but we should always be on guard against citing an isolated critical comment of his without taking into account other pronouncements on the same score. We should weigh them all carefully to see where the real truth lies, to determine in which instances he is reasoning dispassionately and with authority, in which he is merely splenetic. For a simple instance, take these familiar opinions on Chesterfield's letters:

1) 'They teach the morals of a whore, and the manners of a dancing master.'

2) 'It was not to be wondered at that they had so great a sale, considering that they were the letters of a statesman, a wit, one who had been so much in the mouths of mankind, one long accustomed *virum volitare per ora.'*

3) 'Lord Chesterfield's *Letters to his Son,* I think, might be made a very pretty book. Take out the immorality, and it should be put into the hands of every young gentleman.'

Who can be in serious doubt which of these three represents Johnson's considered critical opinion? And when we remember that the first remark was made at a time when he was still wounded at Chesterfield's coldness over the *Dictionary,* it is easy to understand why the moment was hardly propitious for objective criticism.

A deal has been said and written both before and after Lord Macaulay, that brilliant and brazenly prejudiced decrier of prejudices not his own, about several prejudices of Johnson's—the most notable instances, Milton, Swift, and Gray. Thanks to Boswell, Hawkins, Mrs. Thrale, Fanny Burney, we know more of the complex workings of Johnson's personality than of any other man who ever lived. We can fit most of these 'critical sins' into

---

[1] Sir Walter Raleigh is a conspicuous exception.

their context and supplement our analysis of his critical position by a knowledge and understanding of this personal element; consequently we can often understand and explain, though we cannot always excuse, his mistakes in judgment.

Three deep-seated personal traits are of the utmost importance to a full appreciation of Johnson's criticism: his dislike of imitations, his obstinate persistence in a challenged opinion, and, most important of all, his detestation of exaggerated praise. The first of these is evident in his criticism (particularly of pastorals and contemporary ballads) and has been frequently pointed out, so I shall not discuss it here; but the other two have not, I think, been sufficiently emphasized.

'The drawback to his character,' wrote Sir Joshua Reynolds, 'is entertaining prejudices on very slight foundations; giving an opinion, perhaps, first at random, but from its being contradicted he thinks himself obliged always to support it, or, if he cannot support, still not to acquiesce.' Boswell's conversational tactics too often intensified rather than ameliorated this tendency. Persistence in a challenged, *often random,* opinion is occasionally responsible for Johnson's manoeuvring himself into a false position and in part explains some of his contradictory comments on such subjects as Percy's *Reliques,* ballads in general, and one ballad in particular, *Chevy Chase.*[2] To any one well acquainted with Johnson the motivation in such instances is usually perfectly clear; it is a waste of time to dwell upon it or hold it up to ridicule.

But the personal characteristic of Johnson's most important to consider in any genuine attempt to understand his critical dicta is his intense dislike of 'hyperbolical praise.' He was perfectly conscious of it himself. He once remarked to Mrs. Thrale: 'Why, madam, you often provoke me to say severe things, by unreasonable commendation. . . . I know nobody who blasts by praise as you do.' It is this which provoked Johnson, an ardent admirer of Dryden, to attack his poetry when Garrick was 'extolling in a rapture,' finding sixteen faults in a passage he himself had previously commended. The company was amused that Garrick should catch Johnson out; but is there real inconsistency? In commending the passage Johnson probably felt that its poetic

---

[2] See pp. 43-6, below. Johnson's dislike of 'unreasonable commendation' also influenced his opinion of ballads.

virtues far outweighed its faults, a certain number of which one must usually take for granted, since poets are human. But in the second instance, in pointing out the sixteen faults, he is not really attacking Dryden, but Garrick and Garrick's contention that the passage represents not just fine poetry, but perfection.

Such instances could be multiplied, and they are not limited to his conversation. This dislike of excessive praise explains his occasional slurs on Chaucer. It, together with his dislike of pastoral imitations, is responsible for his notorious censure of *Lycidas* and Milton's early poems. When we realize that such friends of his as Percy and the Wartons (Thomas Warton edited Milton's early poems) were enthusiastically 'discovering' the poetic beauty of Milton's minor works and were rather inclined to rapture on the subject, our sympathies may be with them and against Johnson, but at least Johnson's attack and one of the reasons for it become quite understandable. Though in his *Life of Milton* he dismisses the sonnets so cavalierly, he knew them well, at least one by heart. 'We were puzzled about one of the sonnets, which we thought was not to be found in Newton's edition, and differed from all the printed ones. But Johnson cried, "No, No!" repeated the whole sonnet instantly, memoriter, and shewed it us in Newton's book.' In reestablishing the balance of praise and blame, as he conceives it, Johnson often does himself an injustice.

I have insisted perhaps overmuch on these points, mainly because so many, including several able critics, have shown a tendency to ignore this peculiar character of the great body of Johnsonian criticism, to seize upon one isolated remark or passage uprooted from its emotional context, to ignore other pronouncements that modify it. To that extent they have distorted Johnson's true critical significance.

II

This study has in part merely confirmed what scholars have long suspected about Johnson's knowledge of early English poetry; but it has, I hope, done more than that. No Johnsonian will be surprised to find that Johnson's familiarity with Elizabethan drama was sadly limited—that the only dramatist of the period he knew with real thoroughness was Shakespeare, though he did not neglect Ben Jonson. As for Beaumont and Fletcher, those darlings of the late seventeenth and early eighteenth century, the extent and source of his quotations from them indicate not only the slightest acquaintance, but very little interest.[3]

Yet in their estimate of his knowledge of Elizabethan and pre-Elizabethan literature, both prose and verse, apart from drama, several writers on Johnson have taken far too much for granted,[4] as this investigation proves.

By present-day standards Johnson was hardly more than a dabbler in Old and Middle English studies. Judged by the eighteenth century knowledge of those fields, however, he was certainly acquainted with Old and Middle English, and he had the antiquarian's interest in them. Though he was not an Old English scholar, like the Spellmans, Gibson, Hickes, Lye, or even Warton, he was an amateur student and an enthusiastic promoter of a study he considered extremely valuable.

His acquaintance was usually at second hand, and with Old English poetry negligible; but with some of the prose, the *Peterborough Chronicle,* the *Boethius* of Alfred, the Old English Gospels, more extensive; and when we reach such Middle English prose works as those of Trevisa, Mandeville, and Wycliff, he is definitely on surer ground. Of Langland and Occleve he makes no mention; but he had more than a bowing acquaintance with Robert of Gloucester, Gower, and Lydgate, and while he did not share Dryden's enthusiasm for Chaucer, there can be no doubt, despite certain reactions against 'hyperbolical encomiums,' that he knew and admired Chaucer. That his admiration was qualified we

---

[3] I give no references for this and the following paragraphs, since they are merely a brief summary of the body of the text, which is annotated.

[4] Among others: 'There is very little more [than his blunders] in the *Dictionary* worth knowing. . . . He was no etymologist and knew little of any Elizabethan authors except Shakespeare and Ben Jonson—two fatal handicaps.' Hollis, *Dr. Johnson,* 1928, p. 63.

'With respect to his reading in English literature, we may assert without fear of contradiction that it was exhaustive in those periods in which one might suppose him to be well equipped, that is to say, in the preceding century and a half. He never revealed any genuine acquaintance with the literature before Shakespeare, nor the drama contemporary with him. With Spenser he was of course acquainted. This unfamiliarity with the lesser details of English literature merely proves that he took little share in the new antiquarianism which was to perform the service of rendering the more obscure portions of our literature available to the public.' Houston, *Doctor Johnson,* 1923, p. 40.

may attribute in part to his having to read Chaucer in Urry's very faulty text.

His opinion of ballads has been too frequently misconstrued. An occasional harsh criticism is often held up to ridicule by those more interested in revealing 'the great Johnsonian hoax' perpetrated by a coalition led by Boswell than in trying to understand the true nature of his opinion on ballad literature. No one can maintain that Johnson was an enthusiastic admirer of the ballad, that he ranked it as great poetry, or that he helped to make possible the *Ancient Mariner* or *La Belle Dame sans Merci*. But it is absurd to go to the other extreme. Johnson enjoyed ballads when he was allowed by his friends to take them for unpretentious poetry, and he quoted from them[5] and knew more about them than is generally supposed, as his friends and his own works, including the *Dictionary,* bear witness. His quarrels with Bishop Percy and his occasional ridicule are overemphasized at the expense of his genuine and continued encouragement of the *Reliques*.

Of the early sixteenth century poets of the Scottish school he knew only that they were there, but of Barclay's *Ship of Fools* and *Eclogues* he certainly knew all that is necessary for any save an authority to know. He was very familiar with Sir Thomas More's poetry as well as prose (and Roper's *Life*) ; he had dipped into Skelton with distaste and skimmed through Tottel's *Miscellany*. Sackville he ignored, except for bare mention, but he knew something of Gascoigne. With several prose writers of the period, notably Fisher and Ascham, he was well acquainted.

We must always bear in mind, too, that in the *Dictionary* he specifically states that he intends to make few excursions beyond Sidney (since early writers are, obviously, not the best examples for a standard of modern usage) ; that he made so many, despite this resolve, is strong evidence of his interest in pre-Elizabethan literature.

Several of the contemporaries of Spenser and Shakespeare Johnson never, or scarcely ever, mentions : but for the most part those he refers to he knew thoroughly. His acquaintance with

---

[5] He quotes from *Johnny Armstrong, Chevy Chase, Ballad of King Leir, The Children in the Wood, The King and the Miller, A Prince of England's Courtship of the King of France's Daughter,* the *Robin Hood* cycle, etc.—several times from memory.

Latimer, Raleigh, Knolles, Hooker, Bacon, and Sidney's *Arcadia* was extensive and genuine. He quotes from Wilson's *Art of Rhetoricke,* and he knew something about Painter's *Palace of Pleasure.* Spenser and Shakespeare themselves, of course, he knew very well indeed, except for Shakespeare's non-dramatic poetry. Of the innumerable Elizabethan sonnet sequences we can state positively only that he was familiar with (and quotes from) Spenser's *Amoretti* and Sidney's *Astrophel and Stella,* and that in all probability he did not know Shakespeare's sonnets, which were generally neglected by editors of Shakespeare until Malone. He was extremely fond of Thomas Tusser's quaintly versified agriculture, of Drayton's *Polyolbion, Quest of Cynthia,* and *Nymphidia,* particularly the last, and of Sir John Davies' *Nosce Teipsum,* which he quotes not only in the *Dictionary* but in his *Life of Sir Thomas Browne* and in his notes on Shakespeare, and to which he refers in his *Lives of the Poets.* He quotes occasionally from Aleyn, Taylor the Water Poet, Joseph Beaumont, Corbet, Bishop Hall, Daniel, Sir John Harington, and several times from one poem of Marlowe's and one of Raleigh's. He knew something of Phineas Fletcher, of the verse translations of the late sixteenth and early seventeenth centuries—including particularly Chapman's Homer. There are, of course, several startling gaps, quite apart from drama—Marlowe (with the exception of the one poem mentioned above), Herrick, Campion; but the evidence is merely negative. Failure to mention or quote from a writer may indicate lack of interest, but not necessarily lack of knowledge.

We cannot attribute this lack of interest in Herrick and Campion to any distaste for lyric poetry. The frequency of Johnson's quotations testifies to his fondness for the songs of Ben Jonson, and, surprising to those who do not weigh carefully enough the intent of the well known passages in the *Life of Cowley,* definite predilection for the songs, as well as the satires and epicedes of John Donne.

Despite the handicap of a very restricted musical sense (not to be greatly wondered at in a man suffering from physical infirmities of eye and ear),[6] Johnson was not immune to the

---

[6] Johnson's prose and his couplets, at their best, show that he had an ear for cadence and harmony, if not for melody.

charm of purely lyric poetry, though he was much less susceptible
to its musical than to its emotional and imaginative appeal. In his
notes on the *Tempest* he is led into what is obviously half-hearted
support of Gildon against Warburton for the familiar reason:
Warburton's praise of Ariel's songs is to him suspiciously rhap-
sodic. However that may be, he certainly delighted in the humor
and play of fancy in Drayton's Pigwiggin, as well as in the more
profound imagination of Shakespeare.

The small boy so terrified at the Ghost in *Hamlet* that he ran
up the basement stairs to clutch at the reality of the passersby
grew into the man who literally suffered unendurably over the
deaths of Desdemona and Cordelia; who, when his own end was
approaching, recited with terrible intensity of feeling Claudio's
powerfully imaginative portrayal of the disintegration of death
and Belial's echo of that same speech in Milton's Hell. Such a
man brought far more to the reading of Shakespeare and other
poetry than an admirable common sense and a deficient ear.

In fact, limited though it was, Johnson's imagination was so
great along some lines that he felt he had to apologize to Percy
for being overfond of romances. He was on guard constantly
against the seductiveness of the world of illusion, where great
truths may be imaginatively revealed, but also where true values
may become dangerously confused, where man's recognition of
the stain on his soul in the eyes of God may become exaggerated
to the unbearable proportions of Faustus' last soliloquy. This is
one reason why he took refuge in company and conversation,
keeping Mrs. Thrale up till the early hours of the morning to
make prodigious quantities of tea while he talked.

In many ways an eighteenth century Coleridge, Johnson uttered
in his *Rasselas* from the depth of his own experience a warning,
to which Coleridge himself might profitably have given ear,
against the dangerous prevalence of the imagination unre-
strained by reason and a firm grasp on reality.

III

Johnson was a scholar and a friend of scholars, an omnivorous
reader and a lover of books; but he shared with Pope and Swift
a strong dislike for the pedant and the collector of books for
rarity alone. 'Dr. Johnson . . . almost always prefers the com-

pany of an intelligent man of the world to that of a scholar,'
wrote Fanny Burney. It is not necessarily a reflection on friends
like Oldys, Farmer, Warton, Malone, Steevens that he ridiculed
pedantry, or that he sometimes wrote satirically of book collectors. His inherent vigor of mind and common sense caused him
to realize the danger of collecting for collecting's sake, to rebel
against any unreasonable veneration of the past. He writes in the
Rambler characteristically:

'No place affords a more striking conviction of the vanity of
human hopes, than a publick library; for who can see the wall
crowded on every side by mighty volumes, the works of laborious
meditation, and accurate inquiry, now scarcely known but by the
catalogue, and preserved only to increase the pomp of learning. . . .'

'The learned often bewail the loss of ancient writers whose
characters have survived their works; but, perhaps, if we could
now retrieve them, we should find them only the Granvilles,
Montagues, Stepneys, and Sheffields of their time, and wonder
by what infatuation or caprice they could be raised to notice.'

Again, in his satire on collectors in the *Rambler*: 'This search
he had pursued so diligently, that he was able to shew the deficiencies of the best catalogues. He had long since completed his
Caxton, had three sheets of Treveris unknown to the antiquaries,
and wanted to a perfect Pynson but two volumes. . . . Hirsutus
*had no other reason for the valuing or slighting a book, than
that it was printed in the Roman or the Gothick letter,*[7] nor any
ideas but such as his favourite volumes had supplied; when he
was serious he expatiated on the narratives of "Johan de Trevisa," and when he was merry, regaled us with a quotation from
the "Shippe of Foles." '

Johnson was at times dogmatic, but seldom pedantic; and while
not so great a scholar as several of his contemporaries, he was
a man of wide knowledge and master of what he knew. In reading his satires on pedantry, we should remember another statement, equally characteristic: 'All knowledge is of itself of some
value. There is nothing so minute or inconsiderable, that I would
not rather know it than not.'

[7] Italics my own.

Such a credo carries the more weight when we find it so completely reinforced by his literary career. Surely few men have had a more disinterested desire to know, though many have surpassed Johnson in the amassing of knowledge. His intellectual curiosity was insatiable and catholic in extent. He wanted to know how a farmer thatched his house; he wanted to know from Boswell as many anecdotes about Corsica as that Paolist could supply. Had the Saxons any gold coin? Had Fanny Burney read Norris' *Theory of Love*? She laughed, 'staring a little.' It was worth reading. Indeed, to the average reader of Boswell, who may have the impression that Johnson's conversation consisted primarily in making dogmatic and ponderous answers to frequently impertinent questions, it would be surprising to know how many questions Johnson himself asked—particularly in his letters and on his travels. If his interests had not been so catholic, had been more limited to literature, he would have been a finer scholar, but not so great or so interesting a man.

Fortunately, he was not only a writer but a literary man; he was one of our most devoted lovers of literature, which was to him as much a passion as a profession. It is this, largely, which redeems the scholarly weaknesses of his *Shakespeare*, by far the best edition which had appeared till his time. Deficient of course in many respects, it is none the less a clarification of the whole editorial problem, an essentially sound and invaluable contribution to the study of Shakespeare. And it is this passion for literature and language which makes his herculean hack-work task, the *Dictionary,* if no real contribution to etymology, still an amazing and unique single-handed achievement. It was acclaimed on its appearance in terms of eulogy which may seem exaggerated to those of us who possibly find it chiefly remarkable for amusing blunders, forgetting that it exerted a profound influence in a cultivated and intelligent age, that it gave new dignity to the English language. An approximation of what it meant (and deservedly) to the eighteenth century would be a combination of the *New English Dictionary* and Fowler's *Modern English Usage.*

Johnson's scholarly method is no model; it is often deficient. He toiled prodigiously though sporadically as that 'harmless drudge,' the lexicographer; but he lacked the tireless patience, the meticulous pursuit of facts of, say, an Oldys. He frequently was content with what was nearest his hand; he made mistakes; he left gaps. 'Dipping into' Tottel he quotes half a poem, seemingly under the impression it is the whole—simply because he neglects to turn the page. He is satisfied to glean casual quotations from Camden, to take his Beaumont and Fletcher illustrations from the notes in the edition of Shakespeare he happens to be using, instead of going to the sources.

No one was more aware of these shortcomings than Johnson himself; he acknowledges them candidly. And he by no means always chose the easier path. One of the most surprising things about his *Dictionary* is the pains he took to be accurate, to cull the best and most representative of quotations. We must remember that it was not a scholarly performance undertaken at leisure and in the ease of academic seclusion, but a task completed under pressure of financial difficulties, publisher's complaints, and a constitutional apathy.

Johnson laughed in his elephantine fashion at the collector of rare leaves from incunabula; yet bibliography and the actual craft of bookbinding enthralled him. So much so that Baretti complained of him on his travels in France, 'During our Journey to and from Paris he visited five or six libraries, which is the most idle thing a Traveller can do, as they are but to be seen cursorily. . . .' Both his French and Welsh *Journals* are filled with bibliographical observations. A few quotations will show their nature and extent:

'Oct. 24. We visited the King's Library. I saw the Speculum humanae Salvationis rudely printed with ink sometimes pale, sometimes black, part supposed to be with wooden types, and part with pages cut on boards. The Bible supposed to be older than that of Mentz in 62, it has no date; it is supposed to have been printed with wooden types. I am in doubt; the print is large and fair in two folios. Another book was shewn me supposed to have been printed with wooden type, I think Durandi Sanctuarium in 58. This is inferred from the difference of form sometimes seen in the same letter, which might be struck with different puncheons. The regular similitude of most letters proves better that they are metal. I saw nothing but the Speculum which I had not seen, I think, before.'

'Mr. Bryant shewed me the Library [at Blenheim] with great civility. *Durandi Rationale,* 1459. Lascarus' *Grammar* of the first edition, well printed, but much less than the later editions. The first *Batrachomyomachia.*'

'I lived at the Benedictines, meagre day. Soup meagre, herrings, eels, both with sauce. Fryed fish. Lentils, tasteless in themselves. In the library, where I found Maffeus Historia Indica, Promontorium flectere, to double the cape. . . .' Either the Benedictine library was poor, or the tasteless dinner had dulled Johnson's appetite for browsing as well as eating. This deep interest in bibliography had its best field for operation in the 'forties when he assisted Oldys in the examination and cataloguing of the magnificent Harleian collection of printed books; but, as the above quotations show, it was an interest that remained with him till the end of his life.

He left at his death an interesting list of works he had intended to accomplish, Coleridgean in extent. Among many items it includes :

'New edition of Fairfax's Translation of Tasso, with notes, glossary, &c.

'Chaucer, a new edition of him, from manuscripts and old editions, with various readings, conjectures, remarks on his language, and the changes it had undergone from the earliest times to his age, and from his to the present: with notes explanatory of customs, &c., and references to Boccace, and other authours from whom he has borrowed, with an account of the liberties he has taken in telling the stories; his life, and an exact etymological glossary.

'History of the Revival of Learning in Europe, containing an account of whatever contributed to the restoration of literature. . . .

'History of Criticism, as it relates to judging of authours, from Aristotle to the present age. An account of the rise and improvements of that art; of the different opinions of authours, ancient and modern.

'Poetical Dictionary of the English Tongue.'

He accomplished none of these. But all his life he encouraged others to increase the world's store of knowledge. Johnson and the Club subscribed to Lye's *Saxon-Gothic Dictionary.* He urged

Sastres on with his *Dictionary*. He tried to persuade Windham to translate Thuanus. Delighted over Nichols' *Anecdotes,* he wrote him, 'I wish you would add your own discoveries and intelligence to those of Dr. Rawlinson, and undertake the supplement to Wood. Think of it.' Similarly, he asked Mr. Seward to 'tell Dr. Harrington that I wish he would publish another volume of the *Nugae antiquae*; it is a very pretty book.' He exhorted Dr. Maxwell to write a History of Ireland. He upbraided O'Connor and Astle for not continuing their researches. Everything, from geographical dictionaries to comparative philology interested Johnson; wind of a new project, or history, or edition, or dictionary was all that was necessary to call forth his enthusiastic support.

But we are more concerned here with a specific type of antiquarianism, the recovery and appreciation of earlier English poetry. In this recovery Johnson took little direct part; but no one appreciated or encouraged more heartily the researches of Farmer in Shakespeare's sources. No one spurred on more eagerly Warton's flagging zeal over his *Observations on the Faerie Queene*. It was Johnson who wrote the Preface to Mrs. Lennox's *Shakespeare Illustrated* and lent the book his full support; Johnson who gave his sympathy and aid to Percy, and Percy's Preface to the *Reliques,* in which from among all his friends he singles out Shenstone and Johnson, is ample testimony of his gratitude to the author of the *Rambler*.

Johnson may not have had all the equipment and training of the perfect scholar; he certainly had the more essential fundamental qualities of scholarship—intellectual curiosity, a sense of proportion, a sound conception of the relation of literature to life. More important, he had a passion for truth and intellectual honesty. If he did not always live up to his ideal, we may remind ourselves of his significant remark to Boswell that a man's departure in practice need not invalidate the excellence of his theory. His Preface to *Shakespeare* and his Preface to his *Dictionary* transcend the scholarly deficiencies in those works.

He was not only scholarly in himself but the cause of scholarship in other men. He had a seminal mind. If many of the seeds he scattered fell on barren ground or produced nothing of lasting value, that does not diminish the power and force of his personality in eighteenth century scholarship. No important figure in English literature has more untiringly and unselfishly devoted himself to the cause of learning; and with all his faults of method and performance, no one has better exemplified the true spirit of scholarship.

IV

There is in all Johnson's work, scholarly, critical, creative, a striking unity, proceeding from the clarity of his mind and purpose, from the integration of personality and age. This unity, which is very important, is sometimes misinterpreted as rigid conformance to rule.

For the most part his critical remarks, spoken or written, represent a definite tradition and set of beliefs. In dealing with them we know where we are—no small help. But it is never wise to jump to conclusions with Johnson. Frequently he surprises us by contradiction, and, more important, by unorthodoxy. We should study his personality, examine carefully the emotional context and circumstances before finally estimating such departures; for we may frequently disagree with Johnson, but we ignore him or laugh at him at our own risk. 'Ah, a neo-classicist!' Bufo cries, and comes smack up against the final demolition of the Unities or the appeal from criticism to nature.[8]

This does not mean that Johnson the critic was unconsciously at variance with his age or hampered by his general body of literary standards. His critical system fitted him excellently; but no system, however essential it is to have one, is perfect; and Johnson was greater than his and did not hesitate occasionally to recognize its weaknesses. Still, with all its shortcomings, it was an excellent system which had been built up in the late seventeenth and early eighteenth centuries, and it gave a decided advantage to Johnson, and to Dryden before him, over the Romantic critics, who, having scrapped it, had to rely on personal taste and imagination; and over Matthew Arnold and contemporary critics like T. S. Eliot, who have been forced painfully to reconstruct some substitute out of the Romantic débris, and consequently dare not depart from their systems for fear the systems

[8] Preface to *Shakespeare*. 'Nature' is not used by Johnson on this occasion in the neo-classic sense.

cannot stand of themselves. Dryden and Johnson are like men who have grown up in the Roman Catholic faith and tradition; Arnold and Eliot like converts late in life. The born Roman Catholic has far greater religious freedom and daring than the convert, who, not being entirely at ease, is reluctant to risk unorthodoxy. The greatness of Dryden and Johnson as critics lies primarily in the natural ease with which they fit into a definite and not-to-be-scorned tradition, which gives them orientation but by which they are not invariably bound.

I

EIGHTEENTH CENTURY LIBRARIES AND JOHNSON'S MANNER OF READING

I N THE year 1777 a committee of three men, representing the forty leading booksellers of London, waited on Dr. Johnson to ask him to write brief biographical and critical prefaces to an edition of the English poets. The year before, a London publisher, John Bell, had begun printing at Edinburgh a similar edition.[1] According to Edward Dilly, it was the inaccuracy of Bell's edition, 'as well as the idea of an invasion of what we call our Literary Property,' which 'induced the London Booksellers to print an elegant and accurate edition of all the English Poets of reputation, from Chaucer to the present time.'[2] This ambitious scheme was never completely carried out. The London booksellers decided that it was not feasible to begin with Chaucer, nor even with Spenser; and Johnson contented himself with suggesting the inclusion of five eighteenth century poets, chief among them Thomson. When we are inclined to wonder at the surprising omissions in the restricted scheme of this edition of the English poets, we must remember that the choice, except in those five cases, was not Johnson's. It is interesting to speculate on the lives he might have written if he had begun with Chaucer instead of Cowley, and it will add to our appreciation of him to learn what material he had at his command for writing critical notes on the earlier English poets.

In forming our estimate of the eighteenth century we should always bear in mind that it was an age, from first to last, thoroughly conversant with Shakespeare, more intimately familiar with Milton than we are today, well versed in Spenser and Chaucer, though appreciation of Chaucer was impaired (until 1775) by a very faulty text. It was an age of curiosity about our early literature, of antiquaries and scholars, of enthusiastic recovery of the past.

---

[1] *The Poets of Great Britain Complete from Chaucer to Churchill,* Edinburg [*sic*], 1776-1783; 109 volumes.

[2] Boswell, *Life,* III, 125. See also Courtney, *Bibliography of Johnson,* p. 130.

In 1710 there was a new edition of Gavin Douglas, in 1715 editions of Daniel and Spenser, an edition of *Tottel's Miscellany* in 1717, of Chaucer in 1721, of Skelton and *Gorboduc* in 1736, the first complete edition of Drayton in 1748, two editions of Massinger, in 1761 and 1779, and so on. The tale is too circumstantial to repeat here. Then there are the countless miscellanies like Mrs. Cooper's *Muses Library* (1737), which contains selections from English poets beginning with Langland,[3] and the remarkable and curious *British Muse* of Thomas Hayward (1738), giving 'moral, natural and sublime thoughts' from English poets of the sixteenth and seventeenth centuries.[4] Saintsbury speaks with acclaim[5] of Capell's reprint of *Nosce Teipsum* in his *Prolusions* (1760), as if he were unaware that Sir John Davies had been edited by Nahum Tate in 1697 and that this work had gone through two more editions (1714 and 1715). Bishop Percy's *Reliques,* which first appeared in 1765, has usually been hailed as the introduction of the ballad into modern literature, though there had been several previous ballad collections. Forty years before the *Reliques,* had appeared a *Collection of Old Ballads,* attributed to Ambrose Philips. Philips' collection (1723-1725), if not so scholarly as Percy's, is varied and extensive. He certainly deserves to share in the fame of Percy's achievement.

But Johnson, and the eighteenth century reader as well, was not entirely dependent on contemporary editions of the older poets. A number of great libraries were accessible. During this period several private libraries were broken up and auctioned off at prices which make the book collector of today gasp with envy. Never again will Caxtons, Pynsons, sixteenth and seventeenth century editions go for such a song. In determining John-

---

[3] The *Muses Library* includes selections from Fabyan, Langland, Gower, Chaucer, Occleve, Harding, Barclay, Skelton, Wyat, Surrey, Bourd, Sackville, Churchyard, Higgins, Warner, Gascoigne, Nashe, Turberville, Sidney, Greville, Spenser, Raleigh, Harington, Chalkhill, Davies, Fairfax, Shakespeare, and Daniel.

[4] The *British Muse* includes selections (varying from 2 to 50 lines) from Daniel, Browne, Rowley, May, Mead, Herrick, Beaumont, Baron, Marlowe, Randolph, Wm. Alexander, Aleyn, Armin, Blener Hasset, Brandon, Brome, Campion, Marston, Shirley, Dekker, Webster, Ford, Glapthorne, Habington, Hall, Heywood, Kyd, King, Lily, Sir David Lindsay, Lodge, Massinger, Middleton, Sackville, Tourneur, etc.

[5] Saintsbury, *History of English Literature,* Macmillan, 1925, p. 354.

son's knowledge of English poetry before 1660 we must look for possible sources of that knowledge not only in the eighteenth century editions, but in the auction lists of the time and in some of the great libraries to which he had access. Johnson was an avid reader, as we know, and it would be difficult to believe that he neglected any opportunity to browse through a well stocked library. 'Sir,' he said to the eager Boswell, 'in my early years I read very hard. It is a sad reflection, but a true one, that I knew almost as much at eighteen as I do now.'[6] This we must take as one of those partial truths which Johnson used at times to emphasize a point he wished to make; for, despite this melancholy statement, it is undeniable that he continued to read and to 'read very hard' until the very day of his death, and equally undeniable that there were many things stored in that capacious memory when he died which were not there fifty—even five years before.

To draw up a list of all the libraries Johnson knew would be difficult, to catalogue them tedious, to prove the extent of his browsing impossible. Still, it will be helpful to mention a few with which he was thoroughly familiar, and to indicate, at least, the rich stores of English poetry he had to draw upon.

To begin, then, with the universities. Several times in Boswell's *Life* we come upon such entries as these: 'Johnson this year [1754] found an interval of leisure to make an excursion to Oxford, for the purpose of consulting the libraries there . . .';[7] 'Some part of this ignorance I hope to remove by my book, which now draws toward its end; but which I cannot finish to my mind, without visiting the libraries at Oxford.'[8] Besides the Bodleian, Johnson had some acquaintance with the libraries of All Souls and Christ Church,[9] the latter especially rich in English literature. He knew, of course, the library of his own college, Pembroke, and certainly that of University College, where he dined whenever he was at Oxford with his friend Dr. Wetherel, the Master; University College, in fact, was 'almost filled' with

---

[6] Boswell, *Life*, I, 516.
[7] *ibid.*, I, 313.
[8] *ibid.*, I, 314 (Letter to Thomas Warton).
[9] *ibid.*, II, 39, 77 (note 1).

his friends.[10] But of all the college libraries at Oxford he knew that of Trinity best. In 1769 he wrote to Thomas Warton, 'Many years ago, when I used to read in the library of your College, I promised to recompence [*sic*] the college for that permission,' which he did by presenting Baskerville's edition of Virgil.[11]

In 1765 Johnson visited Cambridge,[12] probably to see his friend, Dr. Farmer, of Emmanuel College. Johnson, as we shall see later, followed with the deepest interest Farmer's research into the sources of Shakespeare's plays and knew the results of that research before they were made public. It would be hard to believe that during his visits to Cambridge he never set foot in the library of Emmanuel, especially since we see from his knowledge of Milton's manuscripts[13] that he was acquainted with the library of Trinity College; and since he almost certainly stayed with Dr. Farmer while at Cambridge,[14] it is even more probable that he spent some time with Farmer's fine private collection of books. Beyond these conjectures we cannot go. Boswell and Hawkins are silent, and Johnson does not commit himself.

Boswell does, however, give us a detailed account of the interview between the King and Johnson in Buckingham House Library, which Johnson had the privilege of visiting, and toward the formation of which he contributed.[15] In addition to all these, there are the private libraries of his friends to be considered. It is to be regretted that personal prejudice caused him to neglect Garrick's generous offer to let Johnson consult his excellent collection of Shakespeare and Elizabethan drama.[16] But he did not always turn down such opportunities. 'Johnson, during his stay at Langton, had the advantage of a good library.'[17] What this

[10] Johnson, *Letters*, I, 113 and note 3; II, 14-15; Boswell, *Life*, II, 504.
[11] Boswell, *Life*, II, 77 and note 1.
[12] *ibid.*, I, 563.
[13] Johnson, *Lives of the Poets*, I, 164-9.
[14] Boswell, *Life*, I, 599-600, Appendix C.
[15] *ibid.*, II, 38 and note 1. This 'contribution' was only his long letter of advice to Barnard (Johnson, *Letters*, I, 142-7); but it is an extremely interesting letter.
[16] 'I regretted the reflection in his Preface to Shakespeare against Garrick, to whom we cannot but apply the following passage: "I collated such copies as I could procure, and wished for more, but have not found the collectors of these rarities very communicative." ' Boswell, *Life*, II, 220-1.
[17] *ibid.*, I, 551.

library contained we do not know; but such statements by Boswell show clearly how much importance Johnson attached to the privileges of a library wherever he happened to be staying. Usually, when he visited Oxford he went out to Elsfield to pay his respects to Wise, the Radcliffe Librarian. 'Here,' again Boswell notes, 'was an excellent library; particularly, a valuable collection of books in Northern literature, with which Johnson was often very busy.'[18] Even that gay dog, Topham Beauclerk, was a collector of books.[19]

The most interesting and provocative of speculation among the libraries of his close friends to which Johnson had access were those of the two brothers, Joseph and Thomas Warton—both scholars, both poets and interested in England's heritage of early poetry. Johnson knew them intimately; with both he maintained a correspondence. He probably spent some time at least in the library of Thomas Warton, whom he used to visit when at Oxford. There he would have found the works of Lord Brooke (1633), Browne's *Pastorals* (1613), Gower's *De Confessione Amantis* (1532), the 1617 edition of Spenser, the works of Taylor, the Water Poet (1630), Harington's *Orlando Furioso* and *Epigrams* (1634), Gascoigne's *Droome of Droomesday* [*sic*] (1586), Aleyn's *History of Henry VII* (1638), Shirley's *Poems* (1646) and *Plays* (1653), the 1559 edition of the *Myrrour for Magistrates,* a sixteenth century edition of *Piers Ploughman,* and other treasures of English poetry.[20] There is, of course, no evidence as to which of these books Johnson read, no definite proof that he read any of them at all; there is only the strong probability.

The greatest library of the eighteenth century, however, was that of Harley, Earl of Oxford, and this library (or at least half of it) Johnson had occasion to know well. It is impossible to determine with perfect exactness the extent of his share in the cataloguing of the Harleian Collection of Printed Books, and in the publication of the *Harleian Miscellany.* Boswell's information is meagre and unsatisfactory on this point. Hawkins is more

---

[18] Boswell, *Life,* I, 317.

[19] Hawkins, *Life,* p. 422. At his death the sale of his library brought five thousand pounds.

[20] *A Catalogue of Books,* London, Thomas Payne, 1801. This catalogue includes the books of Joseph Warton as well. With these Johnson was most probably not familiar.

detailed, but his views on the matter, as he admits himself, are largely conjectural. Subsequent writers merely cloud the issue.

In 1742 a London bookseller, Thomas Osborne, bought the collection of printed books which had formerly belonged to the Earl of Oxford.[21] Osborne's purpose was a purely business venture. He immediately planned to catalogue the books for sale and for that end procured the services of Michael Mattaire, who drew up the scheme of arrangement for the *Catalogue* and wrote the Latin dedication. As editors Osborne chose Johnson and William Oldys. Johnson wrote the *Proposals for printing Bibliotheca Harleiana,* possibly the Preface to Volume III; also the *Proposals* for printing the *Miscellany,* as well as the Preface to the *Miscellany.*[22] According to Boswell, Johnson wrote the Latin accounts of the books in the *Catalogue.* According to Hawkins,[23] he wrote *all* the accounts in the third and fourth volumes, having been hired by Osborne as a substitute for Oldys, who was 'hindered by the restraint of his person in the Fleet, a misfortune that he laboured under some time about that period.' A third view[24] is that Johnson wrote the bibliographical remarks in the first two volumes, Oldys being responsible for the third and fourth.[25]

Obviously, Johnson's share in the *Catalogue,* apart from the *Proposals* and Preface, is a matter of sheer conjecture. The varying accounts are confusion worse confounded; all evidence I have found, save Boswell's and Hawkins', may safely be thrown out of court.[26] Of these two Hawkins' testimony seems the less credible.[27]

[21] *A Literary Antiquary, Memoir of William Oldys,* pp. xxii-xxv.

[22] Boswell, *Life,* I, 177, 178, 202.

[23] Hawkins, *Life,* p. 133.

[24] *A Literary Antiquary,* p. xxiv.

[25] *Catalogus Bibliothecae Harleianae* was printed, not all at once, but over a period of two years—Volumes I and II came out in 1743, Volumes III and IV in 1744; Volume V came out in 1745—it is simply a catalogue of Osborne's own remainders. See also Courtney, *Bibliography of Johnson,* p. 13.

[26] Nathan Drake, in his *Essays, Biographical, Critical, and Historical,* draws his material indiscriminately from Boswell and Hawkins; for instance, in his account of Oldys (I, 71) he is following Hawkins; while in his life of Johnson (I, 154) he follows Boswell's conflicting version—seemingly aware of no discrepancy. In a *Literary Antiquary* the author draws his material (again demonstrably) both directly from Boswell and Hawkins, and indirectly from them through Drake—with a little Murphy thrown in for good measure.

[27] Hawkins' whole position is tenuous. 'At what part of the catalogue Oldys's

The only way to cut the knot is with Johnson's sword of common sense. Of one thing there can be no doubt; both Johnson and Oldys worked on the *Catalogue*—probably together. Any further conjecture, if more skilfully eclectic, is still no better than the naïve hodgepodge of Nathan Drake or the compiler of a *Literary Antiquary*.

The *Harleian Miscellany* presents a similar problem, unless we ignore Hawkins and accept the statement of the more accurate Boswell that Johnson wrote the *Proposals* and the Introduction, an *Essay on the Origin and Importance of Small Tracts and Fugitive Pieces*;[28] while the actual selection of the pamphlets to be printed was left to Oldys. The *Harleian Miscellany,* interesting as it is, does not concern us here. Apart from the reprint of John Bale's *Iohan Baptystes* (Volume I) and *Brefe Chronycle of Sir Iohan Oldcastle* (Volume II), and Skelton's *Elynour Rummin: the famous Ale-Wife of England* (Volume I), there is nothing in the *Miscellany* which comes within the scope of this essay; and Johnson's knowledge of Skelton is proved on other grounds, while his knowledge of John Bale remains one of many possibilities impossible to prove. The *Preface,* however, is good reading and further evidence of Johnson's interest in all types of English literature.

The *Catalogue* is another matter. When one reads through the list of books in that great collection and thinks of Johnson picking many of them up, examining them, describing them, and skimming through their pages, one feels on the verge of an important discovery, direct proof of which is disconcertingly lacking. It is certain that hundreds of those books passed through his hands, but which ones and how much he read of them we shall never know. That he read some, and that this was probably the

labours ended and Johnson's begin I have no express authority for saying: It is related of Johnson, by a person who was very likely to know the fact, that he was employed by Osborne to make "a catalogue of the Harleian Library." . . . This is one of the facts on which I ground my assertion that Johnson worked on the catalogue: to discriminate between his notes and those of Oldys, is not easy.' Hawkins, *Life,* pp. 133-4.

Hawkins fails to mention Oldys at all in connection with the *Miscellany,* which, he mistakenly says, was published in 1749. It first appeared 1744-1746.

[28] In the first issue Johnson's essay did not have this title. Courtney, *Bibliography of Johnson,* p. 15.

cause of friction between him and Osborne, is borne out by Boswell's story of Johnson's knocking Osborne down with a folio,[29] and by an even more significant anecdote: 'He paused occasionally to peruse the book that came to his hand. Osborne thought that such curiosity tended to nothing but delay, and objected to it with all the pride and insolence of a man, who knew that he paid daily wages.'[30]

There are in this catalogue numbers of books from which Johnson quotes in the *Dictionary,* and to which he alludes in his other works. But the provocative question is: how much did he know about the other English poets represented in that library whom he never mentions?

Important, too, in connection with his work on the Harleian Collection is his close association with William Oldys, who, in the words of Boswell, was 'a man of eager curiosity and indefatigable diligence, who first exerted that spirit of inquiry into the literature of the old English writers, by which the works of our great dramatick poet have of late been so signally illustrated.'[31] Oldys was one of the greatest of English scholars; he dominated English scholarship during the period 1735-1750. Johnson probably first met him about 1740, knew him intimately for five years and remained his friend until Oldys died in 1761.

When we consider the possible connection between the Harleian library and Johnson's *Dictionary,* the number of years between the sale of the library and the beginning of work on the *Dictionary* seems to preclude the possibility that he was using any of the Harleian books at all. At times he did quote from memory, but such extensive quotation as we find in the *Dictionary* from poets like Aleyn and Tusser could not be from memory. Besides, we know that in most cases 'the authorities were copied from the books themselves, in which he had marked the passages with a black-lead pencil.'[32] Unquestionably Johnson had the actual books

---

[29] Boswell, *Life,* I, 178.
[30] Murphy, *Essay on Life and Genius of Dr. Johnson*—Johnson, *Works,* I, 47.
[31] Boswell, *Life,* I, 202.
[32] *ibid.,* I, 217-18. Boswell, according to the evidence of Hawkins and Percy, is not entirely accurate in his description of Johnson's method. 'Boswell's account of the manner in which Johnson compiled his *Dictionary* is confused and erroneous. He began his task (as he himself expressly described to me), by

in his own possession, whether they belonged to him or were
merely borrowed for the occasion from friends like Birch and
the Wartons.[33] But he might have bought some of the Harley
books at Osborne's ridiculously low prices. We must not over-
look, in all this discussion of libraries, the fact that Johnson
had books of his own. Boswell does not give us many details on
this subject, but he has this entry: 'Mr. Levet this day shewed me
Dr. Johnson's library, which was contained in two garrets over
his chambers. . . . I found a number of good books, but very
dusty and in great confusion.'[34] Hawkins gives a somewhat similar description, adding, typically, that the books were 'chosen
with so little regard to editions or their external appearance, as
shewed they were intended for use, and that he disdained the
ostentation of learning.'[35] He further illuminates one source of
Johnson's library: 'Among the books in his library, at the time
of his decease, I found a very old and curious edition of the
works of Politian, which appeared to belong to Pembroke college,
Oxford . . . and had been used as his own for upwards of fifty
years.'[36] The *Sales Catalogue* of Johnson's library contains six

devoting his first care to a diligent perusal of all such English writers as were
most correct in their language, and under every sentence which he meant to
quote he drew a line, and noted in the margin the first letter of the word under
which it was to occur. He then delivered these books to his clerks. . . .' Percy;
Boswell, *Life,* I, 218, note 1.

'An interleaved copy of Bailey's dictionary in folio he made the repository of
the several articles, and these he collected by incessant reading the best authors
in our language, in the practice whereof, his method was to score with a black-
lead the words by him selected, and give them over to his assistants to insert in
their places. The books he used for this purpose were what he had in his own
collection, a copious but miserably ragged one, and all such as he could borrow.
. . .' Hawkins, *Life,* p. 175.

I quote these passages in full because it is of vital importance in this study to
know, beyond any doubt, that Johnson never left the choice of quotations in the
Dictionary to his amanuenses, but did the reading for them and chose them himself. On this point Boswell, Hawkins, and Percy all agree.

[33] For instances of Johnson's borrowing books for this purpose from Dr.
Birch, Mrs. Strahan, and Andrew Millar, see Johnson, *Letters,* I, 30, 31, 32, 35,
44, etc. Also Hawkins, *Life,* p. 175. Johnson, like Coleridge, frequently neglected
to return borrowed books.

[34] Boswell, *Life,* I, 504-5.

[35] Hawkins, *Life,* p. 452.

[36] *ibid.,* p. 445, note.

hundred fifty items of books—between seven and eight hundred volumes.[37] Is is a most interesting collection.

It was not in his nature to go methodically through all the libraries he knew, or, for that matter, through his own books. He read a great deal, but always in a desultory manner, sporadically, without any definite scheme.[38] It is essential in this attempt to discover, and define so far as possible, his knowledge of early English poetry that we should understand clearly his manner of reading. His acquaintance was wide; the extent of his knowledge of the poets to whom he refers and from whom he quotes is more difficult to determine.

Johnson read, like Coleridge, as inclination led him, believing that what one reads as a task will do little good, and recommending that everyone read at least five hours each day.[39] It was his habit to read whenever he felt like it, often regardless of the company he was in, sometimes to the keen embarrassment of Boswell. He would seize upon a variety of books, suddenly throwing down one and taking up another,[40] reading in a fever of concentration which his friends described as ravenous. He was himself aware of this, for he says: 'I used formerly, when sleepless in bed, *to read like a Turk.*'[41] Fanny Burney gives us an excellent picture of him:

'His attention, however, was not to be diverted five minutes from the books, as we were in the library; he pored over them, shelf by shelf, almost touching the backs of them with his eyelashes, as he read their titles. At last, having fixed upon one, he began, without further ceremony, to read to himself, all the time standing at a distance from the company.'[42]

[37] *A Catalogue of the Valuable Library of Books, of the late learned Samuel Johnson, Esq; L.L.D. Deceased,* London, 1785.
[38] Boswell, *Life,* I, 65-6.
[39] *ibid.,* I, 496.
[40] *ibid.,* III, 271.
[41] *ibid.,* IV, 472.
[42] Tinker, *Dr. Johnson and Fanny Burney,* p. 3. Mrs. Piozzi has an interesting passage in this connection: 'Mr. Johnson had never, by his own account, been a close student, and used to advise young people never to be without a book in their pocket, to be read at bye-times when they had nothing else to do. "It has been by that means (said he to a boy at our house one day) that all my knowledge has been gained, except what I have picked up by running about the world with my wits ready to observe, and my tongue ready to talk. A man is seldom in a humour to unlock his book-case, set his desk in order, and betake himself to serious study:

The voraciousness of his literary appetite is not the only peculiarity about his reading. He had a way of skimming through
books, of never bothering to read them entirely unless particularly
struck by them. In commenting on Twiss' *Travels in Spain,* he
once naïvely remarked that he had not cut the leaves yet, but had
read wherever the leaves were open, and supposed that what
was in the uncut pages would hardly be worse than what was in
the open pages.[43] Even the faithful Boswell was a little shocked
by this idiosyncrasy and took sly pleasure when, after discussing
a new book, Mr. Elphinstone asked Johnson in some surprise:
'What, have you not read it through?' Whereupon the Doctor,
unperturbed, countered, 'No, Sir, do *you* read books *through*?'[44]
The more we learn to know Johnson, however, the more we are
inclined to agree with Mrs. Knowles: 'He knows how to read
better than any one; he gets at the substance of a book directly;
he tears out the heart of it.'[45] He undoubtedly had a rare faculty
for seizing upon the kernel of a book, and with his admirable
memory, once he knew a thing he knew it permanently.

Of this failing, if failing it be, Johnson was himself perfectly
aware. It was, surely, with his own way of reading in mind that
he wrote: 'Many of those who have determined with great bold-
ness upon the various degrees of literary merit, may be justly
suspected of having passed sentence, as *Seneca* remarks of *Claudius*

> Una tantum parte audita,
> Saepe et nulla,

without much knowledge of the cause before them: for it will not
easily be imagined of *Langbaine, Borrichius,* or *Rapin,* that they

---

but a retentive memory will do something, and a fellow shall have a strange
credit given him, if he can but recollect striking passages from different books,
keep the authors separate in his head, and bring his stock of knowledge artfully
into play. . . ." ' Mrs. Piozzi, *Anecdotes,* pp. 36-7. See also *Anecdotes,* p. 166;
Hawkins, *Life,* pp. 16 and 17.

[43] Boswell, *Life,* II, 396.

[44] *ibid.,* II, 260. For similar instances: *ibid.,* II, 101; III, 277-8; IV, 356.
' "Alas, Madam! (continued he) how few books are there of which one ever can
possibly arrive at the *last* page! Was there ever yet any thing written by mere
man that was wished longer by its readers, excepting Don Quixote, Robinson
Crusoe, and the Pilgrim's Progress?" ' Mrs. Piozzi, *Anecdotes,* pp. 179-80.

[45] Boswell, *Life,* III, 323.

had very accurately perused all the books which they praise or censure. . . .'[46]

Such, then, were some of the possible sources of Johnson's knowledge of English poetry, and such was his manner of reading. It is unfair to him to overemphasize the story of the uncut pages; yet we should always remember that Johnson did not invariably read books *through*. His knowledge of a certain book does not necessarily prove that he knew all that is in that book. But we must remember, too, that all the evidence is not available. The most we can hope to do is to discover what poets he definitely knew and, so far as possible, how well he knew them.

[46] Johnson, *Rambler No. 93, Works,* V, 139.

JOHNSON AND NORTHERN LEARNING

871-1380

I T IS not surprising that Johnson, with his all-embracing thirst for knowledge, should have been interested in Old and Middle English literature. We expect to find that he has at least a smattering of Old and Middle English. What *is* surprising is to discover the extent of his knowledge. Johnson was not, and made no pretense to be, an Anglo-Saxon scholar; but he knew far more than we suppose. He was well acquainted with what had been done and what was being done in the study of our parent literature. Chaucer was the morning star to him as to most of us, but Johnson was too good a literary astronomer not to perceive minor constellations in those heavens.

He had all his life a passion for language, which he called the 'pedigree of nations.'[1] As Boswell says, the two subjects nearest his heart were biography and philology.[2] It is true that he never made any direct contribution to the study of English philology; but he was always a generous and enthusiastic champion of philologists and students of early literature, and the study owes him a debt for a lifelong encouragement of its pursuit.

It was a custom, lasting well into the eighteenth century, for members of the two Universities to write poems on great occasions in all the languages studied there. Boswell tells of someone's finding fault with this writing of verses in dead languages and ridiculing in Johnson's presence Oxford and Cambridge for publishing collections of them not only in Greek and Latin, but in Syriac, Arabic, and other lesser known tongues. To this objector Johnson replied firmly, 'I would have as many of these as possible; I would have verses in every language that there are the means of acquiring.'[3]

[1] 'There is no tracing the connection of ancient nations, but by language; and therefore I am always sorry when any language is lost, because languages are the pedigree of nations.' Boswell, *Journal,* V, 255-6.

[2] Boswell, *Life,* IV, 40. See also, Johnson, *Idler No. 84, Works,* VII, 339.

[3] Boswell, *Life,* II, 425.

He was especially interested in all the Teutonic dialects—
Frisian, Gothic, Dutch, as well as Anglo-Saxon—and went to
great pains to learn something about Gaelic (Erse). Boswell
wrote to him from Edinburgh in 1774: 'I have received for you,
from the Society for propagating Christian Knowledge in Scotland, the following Erse Books:—*The New Testament; Baxter's
Call; . . . A Gaelick and English Vocabulary.*'[4] These books
Johnson afterwards presented to the Bodleian Library. Three
years later Boswell again wrote: 'One Shaw, who seems a modest
and a decent man, has written an *Erse Grammar,* which a very
learned Highlander, Macbean, has, at my request, examined and
approved . . . such a work deserves patronage.' And patronage
Shaw received; Johnson wrote a foreword to his *Proposals for an
Analysis of the Scotch Celtick Language.*[5] Similarly, he had previously championed the cause of the Gaelic Bible against severe
opposition—so heatedly, in fact, that he once said, 'My zeal for
languages may seem, perhaps, rather over-heated, even to those
by whom I desire to be well-esteemed.'[6] But for this he had his
reward. During his tour of the Hebrides he had the satisfaction
of being told 'that his name had been gratefully celebrated in one
of the parochial congregations in the Highlands, as the person
to whose influence it was chiefly owing that the New Testament
was allowed to be translated into the Erse language.'[7] Even Boswell
did not escape his linguistic evangelism; he was anxious for
Boswell to compile a dictionary of words peculiar to Scotland.[8]

Johnson's curiosity did not stop here. In 1777 he wrote to
Charles O'Connor: 'I expected great discoveries in Irish antiquity,
and large publications in the Irish language; but the world still
remains as it was, doubtful and ignorant.'[9] He promised to procure some philological works for Mr. Wise, and did succeed in
getting hold of a 'Finnick Dictionary.'[10] He made inquiries into
the Frisian dialect.[11] He and 'the Club' subscribed to Lye's Saxon-
Gothic Dictionary.[12] Shortly before the publication at Oxford of

[4] Boswell, *Life,* II, 319; also II, 326.
[5] *ibid.,* III, 120-2. See also Courtney. *Bibliography of Johnson,* p. 129.
[6] Boswell, *Life,* II, 32.   [10] *ibid.,* I, 320.
[7] Boswell, *Journal,* V, 421.   [11] *ibid.,* I, 550.
[8] Boswell, *Life,* II, 105.   [12] *ibid.,* II, 19.
[9] *ibid.,* III, 127.

King Alfred's Will he wrote to Thomas Astle, the editor, 'Your
notes on Alfred appear to me very judicious and accurate, but
they are too few,' adding, characteristically, 'Had the Saxons
any gold coin?'[13]

Johnson was particularly interested in comparative philology[14]
and eager to learn at least enough of various dialects to trace
resemblances. While in northern Scotland and the Hebrides he
made many inquiries into the language and was somewhat exas-
perated that the natives were able to give so little useful information. He probably had a very slight acquaintance with Icelandic[15]
and with Gothic[16]: and he derived much information from books
like Mallet's *Northern Antiquities,* which was translated and
edited by his friend, Bishop Percy, and which contained a 'description of the manners, customs, religion and laws of the ancient
Danes and other northern nations, including those of our own
Saxon ancestors.' On one occasion, in talking to Boswell, he
recalled that 'between Easter and Whitsuntide, having always
considered that time as propitious to study,[17] I attempted to learn
the Low Dutch language.'[18] His progress was interrupted by a
fever; but he retained a smattering of Dutch, for Boswell reports
a statement of his some years later: '. . . English and High Dutch
have no similarity to the eye, though radically the same. Once,
when looking into Low Dutch, I found, in a whole page, only
one word similar to English; *stroem,* like *stream,* and it signified
tide.'[19] This gives us a good idea of the nature of his own investigations. Obviously, his knowledge in such cases was only super-
ficial; he was interested mainly in the trend and development of
language.

13 Boswell, *Life,* IV, 154.
14 'I have long wished that the Irish literature were cultivated. . . . What
relation there is between the Welch and Irish language, or between the language
of Ireland and that of Biscay, deserves enquiry.' *ibid.,* I, 372-3. See also II,
397.
15 From the Icelandic grammar by Jonas in Hickes' *Thesaurus,* which Johnson
knew, and from the translation of the *Edda* in *Northern Antiquities.*
16 From Hickes, and from Marshall's *Four Gospels* in Anglo-Saxon and
Gothic. He describes Ulfilas' Bible in the Preface to the *Dictionary.*
17 This is a curious admission, when we remember his censure of Milton and
Gray because they were sensitive to times and seasons.
18 Boswell, *Life,* II, 301-2.
19 *ibid.,* III, 266.

The important fact in connection with this essay is that Johnson probably had at least a reading knowledge of Anglo-Saxon and Middle English. On one occasion, before going down to Oxford, he wrote to Thomas Warton: 'I hope he [Wise] will be at Oxford, or at his nest of British and Saxon antiquities.'[20] It was undoubtedly in Wise's library that Johnson made some of his investigations into early English literature. He had studied Hickes; he was sufficiently versed in Old English to criticize at some length and with some acuteness Sir Thomas Browne's essay *On Languages, and Particularly the Saxon Tongue,*[21] though in the course of his critical remarks he makes an unfortunate slip of memory. In the *Dictionary* he relied largely for the Teutonic etymologies on Junius and Skinner, with whom he was well acquainted.[22] In the Introduction to that work, a *History of the English Language,* he quotes a fair amount from Old and Middle English writers. One number of the *Idler*[23] is devoted to a discussion of the development of the language, on which he had previously written in detail in his *History of the Language,* concluding in these words: 'Thus have I deduced the English language from the age of Alfred to that of Elizabeth; in some parts imperfectly for want of materials; but I hope, at least, in such a manner that its progress may be easily traced, and the gradations observed, by which it advanced from its first rudeness to its present elegance.'

While Johnson's interest in Old English was mainly philological and historical and so somewhat outside our province, he did not altogether neglect the literature of those early periods. In 1755 he wrote: 'When first I engaged in this work [the *Dictionary*], I resolved to leave neither words nor things unexamined, and pleased myself with a prospect of the hours which I should revel away in feasts of literature, the obscure recesses of northern learning which I should enter and ransack, the treasures with which I expected every search into those neglected mines to reward my labours, and the triumph with which I should display my acquisitions to mankind. . . . But these were

[20] Boswell, *Life*, I, 335.
[21] *Life of Sir Thomas Browne, Works*, XII, 288-9.
[22] Preface to the *Dictionary*.
[23] *Idler No. 63, Works*, VII, 252.

the dreams of a poet doomed at last to wake a lexicographer.'[24]
Neither time nor the scope of the work permitted him to delve
into Old and Middle English as much as he would have liked.

Johnson, however, knew Alfred's *Boethius* well,[25] and possibly others of the translations for which Alfred was responsible.
He was acquainted with the *Peterborough Chronicle* and with a
Saxon version of the gospels. Of Old English poetry he seems to
have known little. In his *History of the Language* he quotes a few
scattered verses in Anglo-Saxon, with the introductory statement:
'The first poetry of the Saxons was without rhyme, and consequently must have depended upon the quantity of their syllables;
but they began in time to imitate their neighbours, and close their
verses with correspondent sounds.' These verses he quotes directly from Hickes,[26] and in Hickes he could have found a far
more detailed and accurate account of Saxon versification if he
had looked more closely.[27]

The truth is that Johnson was more interested in Old English
prose than Old English poetry. All of his quotations of the poetry
he found in Hickes, whereas for the prose he went to other
sources as well. Even in reading Hickes Johnson evidently
skimmed the pages when he came to the discussion of the poetry.
'Of the Saxon poetry,' he writes, 'some specimen is necessary.'[28]
We get the impression that he troubles himself with this part
of Anglo-Saxon literature mainly because he feels that it must
not be entirely neglected. When we realize the few mediocre
specimens on which he based his opinion, we cease to wonder.
The greatest Anglo-Saxon poetry was unknown to him.

In Middle English he was more interested and better in-
formed. He certainly knew Robert of Gloucester,[29] Mandeville,[30]

[24] Preface to the *Dictionary*.

[25] The consideration of the prose in this connection is a digression, but is justi-
fied, I hope, by the value of understanding the full extent of Johnson's knowledge
of Anglo-Saxon and Middle English.

[26] See Appendix.

[27] Hickes, *Thesaurus*, Part I, 186, 187, *et seq.*

[28] Introduction to the *Dictionary*.

[29] *ibid*. Also quoted under *shrew*.

[30] Introduction to the *Dictionary*. Johnson, *Shakespeare*, 1765, VIII, 343; Johnson, *Shakespeare*, 1773, IV, 522.

Wycliff,[31] Trevisa,[32] and a certain amount of anonymous Middle English verse of the twelfth and thirteenth centuries. It is quite clear from his remarks on the verse of this period that he found it more interesting than earlier verse, because he could better appreciate its relation to the whole subsequent development and continuity of English poetry. He was fully aware that this continuity included the old alliterative verse as well, but he never acquired a sufficient knowledge of that for it to lose for him a foreign nature. He is obviously relieved, in his discussion of early verse, when rhyme and the parent forms of modern poetry are introduced.

All the verse, Old and Middle English alike, except Robert of Gloucester's *Chronicle,* quoted in his Introduction to the *Dictionary* Johnson got straight from Hickes,[33] but this is not true of the prose. Besides Hickes, he used Marshall's *Four Gospels* (1665), Gibson's edition of the *Anglo-Saxon Chronicle* (1692), Rawlinson's edition of Alfred's *Boethius* (1698), and Hearne's edition of Robert of Gloucester's *Chronicle* (1724).[33] Wycliff and Mandeville he read in Lewis' edition of Wycliff's *Bible* (1731) and the 1725 edition of the *Travels.*[33]

Johnson was probably ignorant of the chief glories of Old English poetry.[34] The so-called Caedmon manuscript had been presented to the Bodleian by Junius many decades before; but, though he was familiar with the Bodleian and knew something about manuscripts, Johnson most probably had not come across this, or he would surely have utilized his knowledge. He certainly knew nothing of *Beowulf,* though he might have found it entered in Wanley's catalogue. *Beowulf* was not actually published until the nineteenth century; that he should be ignorant of that poem is only to be expected.

The case is practically the same in Middle English. Johnson probably did not know the *Pearl,* or *Sir Gawayne and the Green*

[31] Introduction to the *Dictionary.*
[32] *Rambler No. 177, Works,* VI, 218; Johnson, *Shakespeare,* 1765, II, 66.
[33] See Appendix. In the *Catalogue* of Johnson's Library (1785): Linquarum veterum Thesauri, a G. Hickerio [sic]—Item 89, p. 6; Robert of Gloucester's Chronicle, Oxon, 1724—Item 369, p. 18; King Alfred's Orosius—Item 12, p. 4; Bedae historia ecclesiastica, Cant. 1644—Item 348, p. 17.
[34] See Nichol Smith, *Warton's History of English Poetry,* pp. 8-9.

Knight, which even Warton fails to mention in his otherwise surprisingly good survey of Middle English poetry.[35] Johnson knew, so far as can be definitely determined, only Robert of Gloucester, the *Sancta Margereta,* and one or two anonymous poems printed by Hickes; but, while he was most probably unaware of the wealth of lyrics in the thirteenth and fourteenth centuries, he realized perfectly that something was being written in the way of lyric poetry during that period. Of the two specimens of Anglo-Saxon verse quoted in his Introduction to the *Dictionary* he remarks that they 'contain apparently the rudiments of our present lyrick measures, and the writers may be justly considered as the genuine ancestors of the English poets.' A little later he says of the twelfth century poems he is quoting, 'the first is a rude attempt at the present measure of eight syllables, and the second is a natural introduction to Robert of Gloucester, being composed in the same measure, which, however rude and barbarous it may seem, taught the way to the Alexandrines of the French poetry.' Johnson was making fair use of the material at his disposal.

As we come down to the fourteenth century, we find that he was familiar with Trevisa, Mandeville, and Wycliff. But we are more concerned in discovering how much he knew about Chaucer's immediate predecessors and contemporaries in poetry—particularly, what he knew of Langland and Gower.

Johnson never once mentions Langland, either to quote from him in the *Dictionary* or to refer to *Piers Ploughman* elsewhere; yet it is difficult to believe that he was entirely ignorant of Langland, who was popular in a minor way throughout the fifteenth, sixteenth and seventeenth centuries. That he should know Trevisa and Mandeville and not know Langland cannot be explained away by the occasional accidental character of his reading and researches. The truth of the matter is that he could hardly have avoided some acquaintance with the author of *Piers Ploughman.* To enumerate all the places he might have learned of Langland would be tedious, but it may be well to indicate a few. Mrs. Cooper quotes ten pages from Langland;[36] *Piers Ploughman* is

---

[35] Nichol Smith, *Warton's History of English Poetry,* p. 22.
[36] Mrs. Cooper, *Muses Library,* pp. 9-19.

frequently referred to and quoted by Hickes;[37] Percy, in his *Reliques,* has an essay *On the Metre of Pierce Plowman's Visions*;[38] and Thomas Warton, in his *Observations on the Faerie Queene* (1754) has a long note on Langland, in which he quotes some ten lines.[39] Warton knew Langland thoroughly; he has another note on him in the Appendix to the revised edition of Johnson's *Shakespeare,*[40] and he had Pope's copy of Langland in his own library.[41]

Of these possible sources, Johnson probably did not know the *Muses Library* of Mrs. Cooper,[42] but the rest he not only knew but knew well. For instance, in his Introduction to the *Dictionary* he quotes several verses of an Old English poem.[43] These verses he copies out of Hickes, and immediately below them on the same page Hickes quotes ten lines from *Pierce Plowman.* Johnson could hardly have failed to glance through them at least. Similarly, Johnson was partly responsible for the publication of Percy's *Reliques;* he certainly did more than skim its pages. It is even more probable that he read with some care Warton's *Observations,* which he encouraged with great enthusiasm;[44] he could hardly have overlooked the lengthy passage on Langland. And while Steevens took the main responsibility for the revised edition of Johnson's *Shakespeare,* Johnson collaborated to the extent of adding a few notes; he was certainly enough interested to read the various contributions of his friends to the Appendix.

That Johnson knew at least the bare facts about *Piers Ploughman* seems conclusive, his unsystematic reading notwithstanding. That he never once refers to it is significant. The most probable explanation is that alliterative verse did not appeal to him; his slighting of Langland is owing to the same lack of interest which made him content with only a modicum of Anglo-Saxon poetry. The probability that he knew Langland, despite the lack of definite evidence to prove his knowledge, shows clearly

---

[37] Hickes, *Thesaurus,* Part I, 196, etc.   [42] See Appendix.

[38] Percy, *Reliques,* II, 260.   [43] *Dictionary,* Sig. d2ʳ.

[39] Warton, *Observations,* 89-92, footnote.   [44] Boswell, *Life,* I, 321, 323, 335.

[40] Johnson, *Shakespeare,* 1773, X, Appendix to Vol. II. Warton in his *History* (1774) quotes over 300 lines from Langland; Nichol Smith, *Warton's History of English Poetry,* p. 19.

[41] *A Catalogue of Books,* p. 322, Item 10604.

the danger in asserting positively his ignorance of any poet he does not happen to mention.

We can only speculate over this seeming hiatus in Johnson's knowledge of fourteenth century poetry. With Gower the case is altered. Johnson not only knew Gower but had a remarkably just appreciation of him and of his place in English literature. Gower's fame has suffered long from the epithet Chaucer applied to him in what he considered commendation. It is pleasant to find Johnson writing in 1759: 'In this state, varied a little according to the different purposes or abilities of writers, our language may be said to have continued to the time of *Gower,* whom *Chaucer* calls his master, and who, however obscured by his scholar's popularity, seems justly to claim the honour which has been hitherto denied him, of shewing his countrymen that something more was to be desired, and that *English* verse might be exalted into poetry.'[45]

Johnson's misstatement, that Chaucer called Gower his master, is undoubtedly a result of misreading the familiar passage in the *Confessio Amantis*:

> 'Grete well Chaucer, when ye mete,
> As my disciple and my poete.'

This failure to realize that it is Venus who is supposed to be speaking, not the poet himself, has been common enough; it is not surprising that Johnson fell into the error. Urry, however, in his edition of Chaucer, which Johnson used,[46] quotes these lines with the correct interpretation among the commendatory stanzas in his Preface.[47] Johnson may possibly have been influenced by Edward Phillips: 'Sir John Gowr, a very Famous English Poet in his time, and counted little inferiour, if not equal to Chaucer himself; who was his Contemporary, and some say his Scholar and Successor in the Laurel.'[48] Johnson knew Phillips' *Theatrum Poetarum,* but it is doubtful that he read it before 1759.

---

[45] Johnson, *Idler No. 63, Works,* VII, 254.
[46] See Appendix.
[47] 'Jo. Gower *de confessione Amantis,* Printed by Thomas Berthelette, 1554. Fol. CXC. verso where Venus speaks to Gower:
     "Grete well Chaucer, etc." '
[48] Phillips, *Theatrum Poetarum,* section on Modern Writers, p. 109.

Johnson's praise of Gower, one suspects, was to some extent the result of his distrust of what seemed to him slightly exaggerated popular encomiums on Chaucer; but his admiration for Gower and his appreciation of Gower's poetry were genuine, however influenced by other feelings. It is interesting to note that his appreciation of Gower was in the main an appreciation of his literary craftsmanship and his mastery of English; it is for these very qualities that Gower will probably be remembered longest.

He refers to Gower several times[49] but quotes him only once, in his *History of the English Language.* Gower was well known to the seventeenth and eighteenth centuries. There is a brief account of his work in Winstanley's *Lives,* with a quotation of thirty-nine lines;[50] Phillips refers to him, as we have seen; he is quoted in the *Muses Library;*[51] also in Urry's *Chaucer.* There was a copy of Caxton's *Confessio Amantis* (1483) in the Harleian Collection,[52] and one of the 1532 edition in the Wartons' library.[53] Johnson himself used the edition of 1554.[54]

Johnson could have begun his Prefaces to an edition of the English poets before Chaucer, if he had been called upon to do so. Many important poets and poems he certainly did not know; but his comments on Robert of Gloucester and John Gower would have been most interesting. Though his acquaintance with early English poetry was very limited, he realized where the rudiments of our poetry lay and that the tradition of English verse had continued unbroken from the time of Alfred.

[49] Boswell, *Life,* III, 288; Introduction to the *Dictionary.* See also note 45, p. 36, above.

[50] Winstanley, *Lives,* p. 19.

[51] Mrs. Cooper, *Muses Library,* pp. 19-22.

[52] *Harleian Catalogue,* III, 241.

[53] *A Catalogue of Books,* Item 840, p. 30.

[54] See Appendix. A copy of this edition of the *Confessio Amantis* is Item 583, p. 26, of *A Catalogue of the Valuable Library of Books, of the late learned Samuel Johnson.*

THOUGH Chaucer was dropped from the original plan of the edition of the English poets, if Johnson had lived a few more years he might have left a separate *Life of Chaucer.* An essay on Chaucer in the *Universal Visitor* was at one time ascribed to him, but Boswell was confident, on the basis of internal evidence, that this essay was not among Johnson's contributions.[1] In the interesting list of projected works found among his papers after he died, however, is the note: 'Chaucer, a new edition of him, from manuscripts and old editions, with various readings, conjectures, remarks on his language, and the changes it had undergone from the earliest times to his age, and from his to the present: with notes explanatory of customs, &c., and references to Boccace, and other authours from whom he has borrowed.'[2] Johnson was no Tyrwhitt; his edition would not have been a contribution to Chaucerian textual criticism: but there is no doubt that he would have made, as in his *Shakespeare,* many characteristically sound and valuable critical remarks on Chaucer's poetry.

It is to be regretted that of the comparatively few remarks he did make on Chaucer several are liable to misinterpretation. This is especially true of his comments on Dryden's modernizations: 'The works of Chaucer, upon which this kind of rejuvenescence has been bestowed by Dryden, require little criticism. The tale of the Cock seems hardly worth revival; and the story of *Palamon* and *Arcite,* containing an action unsuitable to the times in which it is placed, can hardly be suffered to pass without censure of the hyperbolical commendation which Dryden has given it in the general Preface. . . .'[3] Again, in speaking of Pope's 'rejuvenescence,' the *Temple of Fame,* he says: '. . . the

[1] Boswell, *Life,* I, 354. See also Courtney, *Bibliography of Johnson,* p. 75.
[2] Boswell, *Life,* IV, 439-40; also III, 288.
[3] Johnson, *Life of Dryden, Lives,* II, 169-70.

original vision of Chaucer was never denied to be much improved
. . . yet . . . as its scene is laid in remote ages, and its sentiments, if the concluding paragraph be excepted, have little relation
to general manners or common life, it never obtained much
notice. . . .'[4]

This disparagement of the *Nun's Priest's Tale* and the *Knight's
Tale* seems, on the face of it, only a regrettable incapacity for
appreciating the best in Chaucer, like his incapacity for fully
appreciating blank verse. But this is not Johnson's true voice.
The man who condoned the anachronisms of Shakespeare and
Sidney could hardly have objected so strenuously to 'an action
unsuitable to the times.' There is another explanation of this
adverse criticism. Johnson's appreciation of Chaucer is not to be
judged wholly by such statements, for in both cases, quite clearly,
he is not writing dispassionately. What has put him on his guard
—even irritated him—is Dryden's 'hyperbolical commendation.'
As I have tried to show in the introduction, Johnson was always
irritated by what he regarded as excessive praise. An understanding of this characteristic is essential to an understanding of his
literary criticism.

His opinion of Chaucer may not have been so high as that of
today or that of some of his contemporaries, but he certainly
admired Chaucer and knew his poetry. What he admired in
Chaucer was his characterizations, the human and the moral
aspects of his work; of this admiration there can be no doubt.
In his Preface to *Shakespeare* he wrote: '. . . *except the characters of Chaucer,* to whom I think he is not much indebted, there
were no writers in English, and perhaps not many in other modern languages, which *shewed life in its native colours.*'[5]

What Johnson did not admire in Chaucer was his versification; but we must remember that he was introduced to Chaucer
in a faulty text. A glance through Speght's and Urry's editions
to a large extent exonerates him. There was no good text of

[4] Johnson, *Life of Pope, Lives,* IV, 175.
[5] Johnson, *Shakespeare,* 1765, I, xl (italics my own). Pope, who also admired
Chaucer, did so for much the same reason: 'I read Chaucer still with as much
pleasure as almost any of our poets. He is a master of manners, of description, and
the first tale-teller in the true enlivened natural way.'—Spence, *Anecdotes,* edited
Singer, 1820, p. 19.

Chaucer, nor appreciation of the true nature of his metre until Tyrwhitt's edition of 1775; and it is impossible to determine whether Johnson knew Tyrwhitt's *Chaucer*.[6] He never once refers to it, or betrays any acquaintance; and, unfortunately, the revised edition of his *Dictionary* was published in 1773, so there is no possibility of finding evidence in a comparison of quotations in the first and fourth editions. For quotations in both he used Urry's *Chaucer* (1721).[7]

Johnson, however, in an early number of the *Rambler* makes a remark which is most interesting in this connection: 'There is reason to believe that we have negligently lost part of our vowels, and that the silent *e*, which our ancestors added to most of our monosyllables, was once vocal.'[8] This remark occurs in a discussion of English monosyllables and Milton's use of them in his poetry. Johnson here seems on the brink of discovering the secret of Chaucer's versification twenty-three years before Tyrwhitt.[9] Unfortunately, there is no sign of evidence that he ever thought of applying this theory to Chaucer's poetry. Probably one of his friends is responsible for this information.

In the Introduction to his *Dictionary* Johnson quotes from Chaucer's translation of *Boethius*,[10] the *Treatise on the Astrolabe*, the *Prologue to the Canterbury Tales*, the *Hous of Fame*, the *Gode Counsaile of Chaucer*, and *Fortune*.[11] There is no reason to believe that he had not read widely in Chaucer; he even quotes from *Adam Scrivener* in his notes on the *Merry Wives of Windsor*: 'Chaucer imprecates on his Scrivener—"Under thy longe lockes mayest thou have the scalle." '[12] In the body of the *Dic-*

---

[6] The only reference of Johnson's to Tyrwhitt I have been able to discover is a reference to his edition of Chatterton—*Letters*, I, 398.

[7] See Appendix. Warton, too, read Chaucer in Urry (*Observations on the Faerie Queene*, p. 123), as did Dr. Gray (Johnson, *Shakespeare*, 1765, Appendix to Vol. V, VIII, Kk3ᵛ).

[8] Johnson, *Rambler No. 88, Works*, V, 107.

[9] Speght was the first to suspect that the secret of Chaucer's verse had been lost; Dryden ridiculed the idea—Preface to the *Fables*—Dryden, *Essays*, edited W. P. Ker, 1926, II, 259, 310-11.

[10] See also *Idler No. 69, Works*, VII, 275, for a discussion of Chaucer's translation of *Boethius*.

[11] Apart from Chaucer's prose, in the Introduction to the *Dictionary* Johnson quotes 287 lines of Chaucer's poetry.

[12] Johnson, *Shakespeare*, 1765, II, 502.

tionary he quotes Chaucer sixteen times—once, despite his seeming objections to it, from the *Knight's Tale*.[13]

This is, in itself, a tribute; for, in drawing up his plan for the *Dictionary*, Johnson states: 'But as every language has a time of rudeness antecedent to perfection, as well as of false refinement and declension, *I have been cautious lest my zeal for antiquity might drive me into times too remote,* and crowd my book with words now no longer understood. I have fixed Sidney's work for the boundary, *beyond which I make few excursions.*'[14] Clearly, absence of quotation from poets of the fourteenth, fifteenth and early sixteenth centuries is no evidence of Johnson's ignorance. It was not his aim to compile a *New English Dictionary,* to cite the earliest instance of certain usages. This explains why it is difficult to trace exactly his knowledge of the poetry of those centuries; and also why he never mentions many poets with whom he was probably acquainted. It is very important not to lose sight of this fact in discussing his knowledge of English poetry before Spenser.

Of Chaucer's two disciples, Lydgate and Occleve, as of his two contemporaries, Langland and Gower, Johnson appears to have known one but not the other. He knew Lydgate and quotes from his *Fall of Princes*, a quotation which he did not find in the *Muses Library*,[15] nor in Urry, Winstanley or Phillips; but which he quotes from Richard Tottel's edition of 1554.[16] He also may have read in Urry's *Chaucer*, Lydgate's *Floure of Courtesie*,[17] *Complaint of the Blacke Knight*,[18] and some verses from the *Prologue to the Story of Thebes*.[19]

Why he never so much as mentions Occleve is hard to discover; he could hardly have escaped some knowledge of Occleve. It is true that he is omitted in the list of poets given by Webbe in

---

[13] Under *donjon.*
[14] Preface to the *Dictionary*. Italics my own.
[15] Mrs. Cooper quotes eight lines from Lydgate—Cooper, *Muses Library*, p. 30.
[16] See Appendix. A copy of this edition is Item 627, p. 27, in the *Catalogue* of Johnson's library.
[17] p. 419—attributed to Lydgate.
[18] p. 451—unattributed.
[19] Commendatory verses—Preface.

A Discourse of English Poetrie, which Johnson knew, and in Winstanley's *Lives.*[20] But among the 'Testimonies of Learned Men concerning Chaucer and his Works' in Urry's edition are sixty-three lines from Occleve. Also, in Camden's *Remains,* a book from which Johnson frequently quotes, is to be found Occleve's *Of Pride and of wast clothing of Lordis mene.*[21] To the modern student of English poetry, Occleve and Lydgate are inseparable and inextricably connected with the study of Chaucer; but Lydgate was far more popular during the sixteenth, seventeenth, and eighteenth centuries than Occleve. There was no edition of Occleve in the Harleian Collection, whereas there were two of Lydgate.[22] The chances are that Johnson knew nothing about Occleve, except perhaps indirectly and in the most casual way.

The Chaucer canon as it was established in the seventeenth and eighteenth centuries was quite different from the canon of today. Milton, Dryden, Pope, and Johnson accepted several poems as Chaucer's which we now know to have been written by other hands. Consequently, in reading Chaucer, Johnson probably read some of those charming poems in the Chaucer tradition written during the first half of the fifteenth century. It is in this connection that we realize the importance of knowing that he read Chaucer in Urry's edition of 1721. Apart from the two poems of Lydgate's which have already been mentioned, Urry's edition contains: the *Coke's Tale of Gamelyn,* the *Testament of Criseyde,* the *Complaint of Criseyde, La Belle Dame Sans Merci,* the *Floure and the Leafe, Of the Cuckowe and the Nightingale,* the *Mery Adventure of the Pardonere and Tapstere,* and the *Tale of Beryn.* The eighteenth century, though wrong in its attribution of authorship, was as familiar with most of the poetry of this period as we are today. Unfortunately, it is impossible to determine how

[20] Winstanley, however, gives a long quotation from Occleve in his account of Chaucer, p. 27.

[21] Camden, *Remains,* pp. 256-61. Mrs. Cooper also quotes from Occleve—Cooper, *Muses Library,* p. 31.

[22] *Harleian Catalogue,* III, 241: *Siege of Troy,* John Lydgate (1513); *Fall of Princes,* John Lydgate (1554).

many of these poems Johnson read; he never once refers to any of them. We must be content with the probability that some of them he knew, despite his habit of skimming pages. At least he knew of the *Floure and the Leafe,* if only in Dryden's version.

At this point it may be well to interrupt strict chronological sequence and consider Johnson's knowledge and opinion of English ballad literature. Some of the ballads and anonymous popular songs he quotes are late seventeenth century, but he was far from being ignorant of our early traditional ballads, and since many of them were composed during the fifteenth century this is, in general, the period to which they belong.

Here again, if one isolates a few remarks of his, Johnson's attitude is easily misconstrued. His knowledge and appreciation of ballads have been underestimated.[23] There can be no doubt that he was genuinely interested in ballads, that he knew something about them, that he encouraged their publication. When Boswell says: 'The conversation having turned on modern imitations of ancient ballads, and some one having praised their simplicity, he treated them with that ridicule which he always displayed when that subject was mentioned,'[24] we must remember that it is not the old ballads Boswell is talking about, but the eighteenth century imitations of them. Anyone who takes the trouble to read a few of these imitation ballads will readily sympathize with Johnson. His hearty dislike of imitations of any kind may sometimes have carried him into error, but it is a wholesome trait.

Just as in the case of the countless eighteenth century pastorals and imitations of Milton and Spenser, he highly disapproved of what he regarded as the exaggerated praise with which many people received these recoveries from the past. There is a deal of sound good sense in his view, especially when we consider the uncritical acclaim with which some of his contemporaries received any new fragment, real or spurious.[25] No one can maintain that Johnson's heart was moved by any genuine ballad 'more than with

---

[23] ' "He loved, he said, the old black letter books. . . ." '—Boswell, *Life,* II, 138, is not, in my opinion, however, a reference to ballads.

[24] *ibid.,* II, 244. See for a similar instance (an account including several of Johnson's parodies) Mrs. Piozzi, *Anecdotes,* p. 45.

[25] For example, Hawkins, *Life,* pp. 389-90.

a trumpet,' yet if his friends had been less overwhelmingly enthusiastic he might have been more so. When he says that a ballad may please the vulgar but not satisfy the learned, nor fill a mind capable of thinking strongly,[26] we deplore the lack of sense of proportion in such a remark; but we must remember Sir Joshua Reynolds' comment.[27] Johnson looked upon ballads as interesting but homely poetry, emanating from the hearts of the common people and owing much of its value to its essential human quality, often moving, but never great poetry. It was only when antagonized by overpraise that he tended to speak of them slightingly. The simplicity of the genuine ballad he appreciated; but he did not believe that simplicity of this kind could be artificially recaptured, or should become a cult.

Exhaustive and meticulous research on ballad literature seemed to him to show a lack of perspective and common sense. 'Cantilenus turned all his thoughts upon old ballads, for he considered them as the genuine records of the national taste. He offered to shew me a copy of The Children in the Wood, which he firmly believed to be of the first edition, and, by the help of which, the text might be freed from several corruptions, if this age of barbarity had any claim to such favours from him.'[28] His satire here is aimed not at ballads, but at pedantry. As a matter of fact, the Children in the Wood happened to be something of a favorite of his; he used it as an illustration simply because he knew it well.[29] The mid-eighteenth century was enthusiastic over ballads. Not only Theobald and Warburton, but Johnson's close friends, Percy, Warton, and Dr. Gray, wrote long and learned notes on ballads as possible sources of Shakespeare and as illuminating his text. It is little wonder that he wearied at times of the ponderousness of those notes.

When he was not asked to take them too seriously he enjoyed ballads. Apart from the Children in the Wood, he had several favorites. Among them were Johnny Armstrong's Last Goodnight and Chevy Chase. The former he knew well enough to

[26] Johnson, Letters, Appendix D (Diary of William Windham), II, 440. The ballad referred to is Chevy Chase, about which see below.

[27] Introduction, p. 3, above.

[28] Johnson, Rambler No. 177, Works, VI, 218.

[29] Quoted in the Dictionary under redbreast.

quote from memory;[30] Boswell once overheard him repeating the refrain to himself during their tour of Scotland.[31] He was very fond, too, of *Chevy Chase,* which he remembered from his college days, if we are to credit an extremely amusing anecdote told by Hawkins,[32] and quotes from it three times in the *Dictionary.*[33] He also seems to have been fond of the song, *Every Island is a Prison.*[34] In all, he quotes nine times from ballads in the *Dictionary,*[35] three of these quotations being added in the revised edition of 1773. Clearly, his interest in ballads, if not over-keen, was steady; and this inclusion of three new quotations in 1773 was not simply the result of Percy's publication of the *Reliques* eight years before, for not one of the additions is to be found in Percy.

To trace in each case the source of Johnson's knowledge of the ballad would be an extremely difficult and none too profitable labor. But one or two facts and surmises are of interest. There are several collections of ballads he might have known, among them Allan Ramsay's *Ever Green* (1724) and *Tea Table Miscellany;*[36] the second of these had run through nine editions by 1738. He almost certainly knew the interesting *Collection of Old Ballads* (1723) attributed to Ambrose Philips, for the first volume contains six of his quotations in the *Dictionary;*[37] and he not only knew, but wrote the Dedication to Bishop Percy's *Reliques.* Those who are inclined to distrust Johnson's appreciation of ballads should remember that he was one of the friends among whom Percy circulated his manuscript collection, and one of the most instrumental in obtaining its final publication, for which we have not only his own word but that of Dr. Percy

[30] Boswell, *Life,* I, 467. Johnson quotes four verses.

[31] Boswell, *Journal,* V, 48.

[32] Hawkins, *Life,* p. 13.

[33] Under *drive, flight,* and *load.* Only one quotation (*flight*) appeared in the first edition; the other two were added in 1773.

[34] Boswell, *Life,* III, 305; V, 291; also, letter to Mrs. Thrale from Skie, Sept. 24, 1773—Johnson, *Works,* IX, 384. This song is by Coffey, and is given in Ritson's *Songs,* 1813; Boswell, *Life,* II, 122 (Hill).

[35] Twice in the Grammar Sec., and under *bravado, drive* (not in first edition), *flight, lamb's wool, load* (not in first edition), *offend* (not in first edition), *redbreast.*

[36] Johnson knew the son of this Allan Ramsay—Boswell, *Life,* III, 283-4—but Ramsay gives versions in Scots dialect, which Johnson never quotes.

[37] See Appendix.

himself.[38] He never quotes from Percy, but he refers to the *Reliques* in a manner indicating close perusal.[39]

Johnson in his notes on Shakespeare shows that he knew other collections of ballads than those mentioned above. He quotes from the *Robin Hood* cycle[40] and from the *Ballad of King Leir and his Three Daughters*.[41] In both cases it is impossible to discover the definite source of his knowledge. The *Ballad of King Leir* he might have read in Philips' *Collection* (Volume II), in the *Reliques*, or in Mrs. Lennox's *Shakespeare Illustrated* (Volume III). The text which he actually quotes in the notes at the end of *King Lear*[42] differs slightly from that given by each of these possible sources; so it is impossible to say exactly from which he was quoting, though it seems most likely that he was using *Shakespeare Illustrated*.[43] Johnson was not himself a student of ballads, but, apart from his own reading, he learned a great deal about them from friends of his who were.

During the second half of the fifteenth century, and the early sixteenth century, except for the ballads, the only really vigorous and lasting poetry was being written by Scottish poets—James I, Henryson, Dunbar, Gavin Douglas, and Lyndsay. It is quite im-

[38] Percy, *Reliques*, I, xiii: 'To the friendship of Mr. JOHNSON he owes many valuable hints. . . .' *ibid.*, Preface, I, ix: 'As most of them are of great simplicity, and seem to have been meerly [*sic*] written for the people, he was long in doubt, whether in the present state of improved literature, they could be deemed worthy the attention of the public. At length the importunity of his friends prevailed, and he could refuse nothing to such judges as the author of the RAMBLER, and the late Mr. SHENSTONE.'

Johnson, *Letters*, I, 89-90. Also *Johnsonian Miscellanies*, II, 68: 'Notwithstanding all the pains that Dr. Farmer and I [Johnson] took to serve Dr. Percy in regard to his *Ancient Ballads,* he has left town for Ireland, without taking leave of either of us.' (Anecdotes by Joseph Cradock.)

[39] Johnson, *Shakespeare*, 1765, VIII, 373, 446. See, however, for what is possibly a quotation, Johnson, *Letters*, II, 328, and note 1.

[40] *ibid.*, VI, 183: '*Adam Bell* was a companion of *Robin Hood,* as may be seen in *Robin Hood's* Garland; in which, if I do not mistake, are these lines [quotes four verses].' Johnson seems to be referring to a collection of Robin Hood ballads. The lines he quotes are to be found, with slight variation, in Philips' *Collection*. See Appendix.

[41] *ibid.*, VI, 160-3; seventeen stanzas quoted. In the revised edition, 1773, IX, the whole ballad is quoted, signed *Johnson*. But the text differs from that in the 1765 edition, and Steevens has the note: 'This ballad is given from an ancient copy in the *Golden Garland*, black letter. To the tune of, *When flying Fame.*'

[42] See Appendix.

[43] This book was published 1753-1754. Johnson wrote the Preface.

probable that Johnson had ever even heard of the *Kingis Quair*;[44] but he knew Urry's *Chaucer*, and so it is possible that he had read the *Testament of Cresseid*,[45] without, of course, attributing it to its true author. Whether or not he knew any other works of Henryson's, and whether he knew anything at all about Dunbar and Lyndsay, is problematical. Allan Ramsay's *Ever Green* contains many poems of Henryson's and Dunbar's. And Thomas Warton in a curious little book called *The Union: or Select Scots and English Poems* (1753) includes the *Thistle and the Rose*, and part of the Prologue to *Sir David Lyndesay's Dream*. This book Johnson may well have seen; one who followed with so much interest Thomas Warton's literary productions must at least have been aware of it. Johnson almost certainly read a tribute of Warton's to the Scottish poets: 'I should be guilty of injustice to merit in particular, and to a nation in general, which amidst a variety of disadvantages has kept a constant pace with England in the progress of literature, were I here to omit the mention of two Scottish poets, who flourished about this time, Sir David Lyndesay, and William Dunbar.'[46] It is reasonable to believe that Johnson had read a little Henryson,[47] and that he at least knew of Dunbar and Lyndsay.

Of his knowledge of Gavin Douglas there can be no doubt. Douglas' translation of the *Aeneid* was well known to the seventeenth and eighteenth centuries. Hickes refers to it frequently;[48] and there was a new edition of his works in 1710. Johnson does not mention Douglas in his essay on English translations,[49] but in the first edition of the *Dictionary* he cites Douglas' authority once.[50] He had a slight acquaintance with Douglas, therefore, as

[44] He may, however, have read *Christ Kirk of the Green*.

[45] There is also a reference to the *Testament of Cresseid* in Hickes' *Thesaurus*, Part I, p. 65, note.

[46] Warton, *Observations on the Faerie Queene*, pp. 234-5. See also Nichol Smith, *Warton's History of English Poetry*, p. 23.

[47] Percy prints Henryson's *Robin and Makyne*, *Reliques*, II, 66.

[48] Hickes, *Thesaurus*, Part I, p. 66 (footnote—quotation of two lines) ; Part I, p. 112—quotation of three lines; Part I, p. 118—quotation of five lines; Part I, p. 138—quotation of twelve lines. None of these lines are quoted by Johnson in the *Dictionary*, however.

[49] Johnson, *Idler No. 69*, *Works*, VII, 275.

[50] Under *deray*. He does not quote here, but the reference is to the *Aeneis*, Book VII.

early as 1755. It may be, as is probably true of Mackenzie's *Lives,* that his attention was called to Douglas by the Scottish amanuenses he employed for the work; he may, like Warton, have learned of Douglas through Francis Fawkes:[51] but there is no reason why he should not have found out Douglas for himself. There is not sufficient evidence to determine whether he used the 1710 edition or an earlier one. Eighteen years later, when revising the *Dictionary,* he cited Douglas' name a second time, as authority for the word *dan,* this time quoting from him.

Curiously enough, the quotation under *dan* in the revised edition, which he attributes to Douglas, is the well known line from Spenser:

'Dan Chaucer, well of English undefiled.'

Why Johnson should make such an obvious mistake is puzzling. He knew Spenser and knew him thoroughly. Besides, this verse was a favorite of his,[52] as it was of Warton's.[53] A search for possible sources of the error reveals nothing definite;[54] and since it occurs only in the revised edition of the *Dictionary,* Johnson was never able to correct the mistake.

Douglas, Dunbar, and Lyndsay were writing well into the sixteenth century. In order to pick up the direct sequence of English poetry, we must return to the last two decades of the fifteenth. Johnson knew Caxton and his contribution to English literature, both as a translator and as the first publisher of Chaucer, Gower, and Lydgate.[55] In the Introduction to his *Dictionary* he quotes a few paragraphs from Fortescue. He knew, too, something about

----

[51] Fawkes published *A Description of May* (Prologue to the XIIth Book of Douglas' *Aeneis*) in 1752. It was Fawkes who probably drew Warton's attention to Douglas—Nichol Smith, *Warton's History of English Poetry,* p. 23, note.

[52] See the well known passage in the Preface to the *Dictionary.*

[53] Warton, *Observations on the Faerie Queene,* p. 96 and p. 141.

[54] Phillips is not responsible. Johnson may possibly have confused Spenser's tribute with a tribute of Douglas' to Chaucer, both of which occur close together in Urry's *Chaucer* and in Winstanley's *Lives;* more probably it was simply a natural slip.

[55] Johnson, *Idler No. 69, Works,* VII, 276: '*Caxton* taught us typography about the year 1474. The first book printed in *English* was a translation. *Caxton* was both the translator and printer of the *Destruction of Troye;* a book which, in that infancy of learning, was considered as the best account of the fabulous ages.' See also *Rambler No. 177, Works,* VI, 217-18; *Shakespeare,* 1765, VII, 547; and Boswell, *Life,* III, 288.

the medieval verse romances; and he had at least dipped into Malory's *Morte d'Arthur*. It is probably true that his slight knowledge of Palmerin and Guy of Warwick[56] came to him through Drayton's *Polyolbion*, of Malory through Ascham's well known censure in the *Schoolmaster*; but his knowledge of Malory went a little deeper.[57] It may be that Warton[58] induced him to glance through the *Morte d' Arthur*. From the same source it is just possible that he knew of Stephen Hawes, who was a 'discovery' of Warton's, and about whom Warton wrote: 'However, in the reign of Henry VII ample amends were made for this interval of darkness by Stephen Hawes, a name generally unknown, and not mentioned by any English compiler of the lives of English poets, but by the accurate Wood.'[59]

Even if he was unacquainted with Hawes, he certainly knew most of the principal writers of the early Tudor period: Sir Thomas More, Fisher, Skelton, Barclay, Wyat, Surrey, and the anonymous poets in Tottel's *Miscellany*[60]—all of whom, except Wyat, he quotes in the *Dictionary*. In common with his age, he was comparatively ignorant of early drama, not only the Miracles and Mysteries, but the work of such men as John Heywood and Raston. Medieval and Tudor drama was not studied, generally

[56] Johnson, *Shakespeare*, 1765, Preface, I, xxxiii; *ibid.*, I, 249.

[57] *ibid.*, IV, 301: 'The story of Sir *Dagonet* is to be found in *La Mort d'Arthure*, an old romance much celebrated in our authour's time, or a little before it. *When papistry*, says *Ascham* in his *Schoolmaster*, *as a standing pool overflowed all* England, *few books were read in our tongue saving certain books of chivalry, as they said, for pastime and pleasure; which books, as some say, were made in monasteries by idle monks. As one, for example,* La Mort d'Arthure. In this romance Sir *Dagonet* is King *Arthur's* fool. *Shakespeare* would not have shown his *justice* capable of representing any higher character.'

[58] Warton, *Observations on the Faerie Queene*, pp. 15-31; 153-5—a lengthy discussion of Spenser's debt to Malory.

[59] *ibid.*, p. 233. Percy quotes from Hawes in the *Reliques*, I, 87-90, referring to the above passage in Warton.

[60] Johnson through Oldys might have become acquainted with Sir Thomas Eliot. Oldys published an abstract of the *Governour* in his *British Librarian*, XLIII, No. V, for May, 1737. A copy of the *Governour* (1531) was in the Harleian Collection—*Catalogue*, V, 337. Johnson probably did not know Lord Berners' translation of Froissart, except by name. He copies Warburton's note, however: 'It would seem so by the title of an old English translation of Froissart's Chronicle, which runs in these words, *Syr John Froissart's Chronicle translated out of Frenche into our Material English Tongue by John Bouchier,* printed 1525.'—Johnson, *Shakespeare*, 1765, VI, 113.

speaking, until the nineteenth century; but of this we shall treat later.

Sir Thomas More was a lifelong favorite of Johnson's.[61] He not only knew More's prose and verse, but Roper's *Life,* and some manuscripts of More's in the Bodleian.[62] As Sir Walter Raleigh pointed out, we can trace in Johnson's notes on Shakespeare his reading in the *Life of Sir Thomas More.*[63] In the Introduction to the *Dictionary* he quotes several pages from More's early poems, a selection from his *History of Richard III,* and his letter to his daughter just before his death. In the *Dictionary* itself he quotes several times from More's poems[64] and twenty-seven times from his prose under the letters E and F alone. Prose and verse he quotes from the 1557 edition of More's works. From Fisher he gives only one quotation.[65] But Fisher, and More primarily, were prose writers; and we are concerned here with poetry.

It is somewhat surprising to find that Johnson knew Alexander Barclay, Skelton's contemporary and rival, though his knowledge of Barclay's dates was inexact.[66] He gives in his Introduction to the *Dictionary* a long selection (ninety-two lines) from the *Ship of Fools,* and his interest in Barclay lasted long after work on the *Dictionary* was finished.[67] In 1754 he wrote to Thomas Warton: 'There is an old English and Latin book of poems by Barclay, called "The Ship of Fools"; at the end of which are a number of *Eglogues*; so he writes it, from *Egloga,* which are probably the first in our language. If you cannot find the book I will get Mr. Dodsley to send it you.'[68] Johnson himself used the 1570 edition of Barclay.[69] In 1774, twenty years after the letter quoted above was written, Warton gave a very full account of Barclay in his *History of English Poetry.*

---

[61] Johnson, *Rambler No. 114, Works,* V, 277.   [69] See Appendix.

[62] Boswell, *Life,* I, 336.

[63] Raleigh, *Johnson on Shakespeare,* Oxford, 1929, p. xxviii.

[64] Under *delectation, eisel, flagelet,* etc.

[65] Under *or.*

[66] Johnson, Introduction to *Dictionary*: 'Barclay wrote about 1550. . . .' Barclay did not die until 1552, but his *Ship of Fools* was printed by Pynson in 1508, and his *Eclogues* were written soon afterwards.

[67] For another reference to Barclay, see *Rambler No. 177, Works,* VI, 218.

[68] Boswell, *Life,* I, 321-2 (Letter to Thomas Warton).

Johnson had a slight acquaintance with another poet of this period, little known even today—Andrew Bourd. He quotes Bourd twice,[70] not in the Introduction, but in the body of the *Dictionary*. On both occasions, however, he quotes from the same passage. The explanation is plain. Those few verses were all he knew of Bourd, and those he found quoted in Camden's *Remains*,[71] not in any edition of the *Boke of the Introduction of Knowledge*.

While Hawes was painfully interring the medieval allegory in an incongruously named poem; while Dunbar and Henryson were writing the last good poetry in the old tradition, and Barclay was translating moral poems into terms 'common and rural'— John Skelton had surrendered to the chaotic state of the English language and was writing verse that was 'rude and motheaten,' it is true, but which had in it some pith. Skelton, the supreme grotesque and buffoon of English poetry, has too often been dismissed either as a curious phenomenon or a vulgar versifier. His fame, however, persisted, though it had ups and downs. In the reign of George II he was still much read; we have Pope's word for it: 'And beastly Skelton Heads of Houses quote.' Skelton's popularity, in fact, was great enough for an enterprising publisher, Davis, to bring out an edition of his work in 1736. It was this which Johnson used.[72] His opinion of Skelton was higher than Pope's, but it is evident that he felt neither great admiration for Skelton, nor special interest in his poetry. In the Introduction to the *Dictionary* he quotes thirty-five lines from the Prologue to the *Bouge of Court* with the perfunctory comment: 'At the same time with Sir Thomas More lived Skelton, the poet laureate of Henry VIII, from whose works it seems proper to insert a few stanzas, though he cannot be said to have attained great elegance of language.' Even if he had not read all the 1736 edition of Skelton,[73] through his connection with Oldys and the

---

[70] Under *cock-on-the-hoop* and *sit*—both in the first edition.

[71] See Appendix. The quotation under *cock-on-the-hoop* has the attribution *Camden's Remains*.

[72] See Appendix.

[73] Lack of complete familiarity with Skelton seems to be implied by the note: 'Dr. *Gray* observes, that *Skelton* has a poem to the memory of *Philip Sparrow*.' Johnson, *Shakespeare,* 1765, III, 414.

Harleian Miscellany, Johnson must have known the *Tunning of Elinour Rummin.*[74] The *Bouge of Court* was an unhappy choice.

Of far greater significance in the development of English poetry than Hawes, Barclay, Bourd, or even Skelton, is the new group of poets in the reign of Henry VIII, headed by Sir Thomas Wyat and the Earl of Surrey. The verses of these two poets were never printed during their lifetime, but circulated in manuscript. It was not until fifteen years after the death of Wyat and ten after the execution of Surrey that some of their poems were finally printed in Tottel's *Miscellany,* along with poems by Nicholas Grimald and 'uncertain auctors.' Tottel's *Miscellany* achieved immediate popularity, running through eight editions in thirty years; and this popularity lasted throughout the seventeenth and eighteenth centuries. Johnson may well have known some of the early editions;[75] but for quotation in the Introduction to his *Dictionary* he used the 1717 reprint of Tottel.[76] He quotes six poems from the *Miscellany,* five of them completely. Of these the first three are by Surrey, one is by Nicholas Grimald, and the other two are anonymous.

The confusion over the authorship of the poems printed by Tottel makes attribution somewhat difficult. We can sympathize to some extent with Johnson when he remarks: 'Of the wits that flourished in the reign of *Henry* VIII none has been more frequently celebrated than the earl of *Surry*; and this history would therefore have been imperfect without some specimens of his works, which it is not easy to distinguish from those of Sir *Thomas Wyat* and others, with which they are confounded in the edition that has fallen into my hands.'[77] Tottel, however, indicates fairly clearly the poems which belong to Surrey, Wyat, and Grimald; a more careful reading would have prevented Johnson's confusion. As it is, he attributes the first three poems correctly to Surrey, but does not mention the authorship of the others. He quotes nothing at all from Wyat anywhere in his works.

[74] See p. 22, above.
[75] There is, however, no copy of the *Miscellany* in the *Catalogue* of his library; he must have borrowed the book.
[76] See Appendix.
[77] Introduction to the *Dictionary.*

Although Johnson seems to have read his Tottel none too closely,[78] he had certainly read in it here and there. He had a passing acquaintance with Wyat, then, but in common with his age he knew Surrey far better. Because of his higher rank, Surrey figures more prominently in Tottel;[79] so it is only natural that succeeding ages came to regard him as being the more important of the two. Johnson never mentions Wyat except this one time, but he does refer to Surrey again. One reason for his greater knowledge of Surrey may have been his friendship with Bishop Percy, who planned an edition of Surrey's poems, which he never published. 'Surrey's *Poems,* the gift of the Editor Dr. Percy to Mr. Warton' is in the catalogue of the Wartons' library.[80] The chances are that Johnson knew of this uncompleted work, either through Percy himself or through Warton.

As for Nicholas Grimald, though he quotes the *Death of Zoroas* as 'the oldest composition I have found in blank verse,' Johnson never mentions him by name. He probably thought this one of the anonymous poems in Tottel. He had never read Surrey's blank verse translation of the second book of the *Aeneid,* though he had heard of it; for in his discussion of Milton's versification he remarks: 'The Earl of Surrey is said to have translated one of Virgil's books without rhyme.'[81] This version of the fourth *Aeneid* was first published in 1554, three years before the *Miscellany.* It was written, of course, several years before, as was Grimald's *Zoroas*; and while Surrey is credited with the first experiment in blank verse, Johnson was not too far wrong in attributing that honor to the lesser poet.

Shortly after the publication of Tottel's *Miscellany* appeared the second and enlarged edition of the *Myrrour for Magistrates* (1563). Among the additions were Sackville's famous *Induction* and *Complaint of Buckingham.* Sackville's *Gorboduc,* written in collaboration with Thomas Norton, had been acted two years

[78] The only one of these poems he does not quote completely is *A praise of his ladie.* He omits the last twenty-eight lines, seemingly unintentionally. It is probable that he simply neglected to turn over the page in Tottel, thinking the poem complete without the lines on p. 146. See Appendix.

[79] Surrey's name alone is on the original title-page. In Arber's reprint of Tottel (1921) his poems occupy thirty pages, Wyat's twenty-eight.

[80] *A Catalogue of Books,* p. 316, Item 10362.

[81] Johnson, *Lives of the Poets,* I, 259. Johnson seems here to be ignorant of Tottel's edition of Surrey's Second and Fourth *Aeneid* in 1557.

earlier, though it was not printed until 1565. A few years later appeared George Gascoigne's two dramatic translations, the *Supposes* and *Jocasta,* his *A Hundred Sundry Flowers* (1573), the *Glasse of Government* (1575), and the *Steele Glasse* (1576).

The eighteenth century was well acquainted with Gascoigne and Sackville. Spence's edition of *Gorboduc* appeared in 1736, and both poets figure prominently in the miscellanies and historical accounts of the age.[82] There was a sixteenth century edition of the *Myrrour* in the Harleian Collection;[83] and the catalogue of the Wartons' library contains Gascoigne's *Droome of Droomesday* [*sic*], and no less than three editions of the *Myrrour for Magistrates.*[84]

When Johnson remarks of Dryden: 'What he wishes to say, he says at hazard; he cited *Gorboduc,* which he had never seen; [and] gives a false account of *Chapman's* versification,'[85] it is only reasonable to suppose that he would not have made such a statement without himself knowing something of *Gorboduc.* He refers casually to this play in the Preface to his edition of *Shakespeare,*[86] and in his notes on *King Richard III* remarks: '*Induction* is preface, introduction, first part. It is so used by *Sackville* in our author's time.'[87] But he never once quotes from Sackville, and does not seem to have been particularly interested in his poetry.

Johnson refers to Gascoigne twice—not to his verse, but on both occasions to the *Notes of Instruction:* 'But this knack [alliteration], whatever be its value, was so frequent among early writers, that Gascoign, a writer of the sixteenth century, warns the young poet against affecting it.'[88] Warton knew a great deal

[82] An account of the *Gorboduc, Jocasta* and the *Supposes* in Percy's *Essay on the Origin of the English Stage—Reliques,* I, 125.

Reference to *Ferrex and Porrex* and quotation from *Induction*—Mrs. Cooper, *Muses Library,* pp. 88-117.

Quotations from Gascoigne's *Araignment of a Lover* (p. 169), *Dan Bartholomew* (pp. 172-3), *Fruit of War* (p. 173)—*Muses Library.*

Reprint of Sackville's *Induction*—Capell, *Prolusions,* Part I.

Various quotations from Sackville in the *British Muse* of Hayward.

Brief accounts of Gascoigne and Sackville in William Chetwood's *British Theatre* (1752), with lists of their dramatic works.

[83] *Harleian Catalogue,* III, 355.

[84] *A Catalogue of Books,* p. 109, Item 3157; p. 320, Items 10521-3.

[85] Johnson, *Lives of the Poets,* II, 110.

[86] Johnson, *Shakespeare,* 1765, I, xliii.   [87] *ibid.,* V, 322.

[88] Johnson, *Life of Waller, Lives,* I, 404. Similarly: 'Gascoigne, contemporary of our poet, remarks and blames the same affectation.'—*Shakespeare,* 1765, I, 165.

about Gascoigne, and it may well be that Johnson's knowledge of his work, however much it was, came through Warton.[89]

Of other poets who wrote during the reign of Mary and the early years of Elizabeth—Churchyard, Whetstone, Tusser, Turberville, Googe, and the verse translators, Phaer and Jasper Heywood, Johnson seems to have known only Tusser and Phaer. He does not quote Phaer in the *Dictionary,* which is hardly surprising, and refers to him only once, but then in a manner implying a fair knowledge of his translation of Virgil: 'The triplet has long subsisted among us. Dryden seems not to have traced it higher than to Chapman's Homer; but it is to be found in Phaer's Virgil, written in the reign of Mary. . . .

'The Alexandrine was, I believe, first used by Spenser, for the sake of closing his stanza with a fuller sound. We had a longer measure of fourteen syllables, into which the Eneid was translated by Phaer, and other works of the ancients by other writers; of which Chapman's Iliad was, I believe, the last.'[90] He then quotes the two first lines of the Third *Aeneid.* Needless to say, Phaer's Virgil is most probably one of the many books Johnson simply opened at random; that he knew Phaer at all is somewhat surprising.

It is perhaps even more surprising to find that Tusser was a great favorite of Johnson's. He quotes Tusser copiously in the *Dictionary,*[91] and continued to read and enjoy him for many years. He knew *Of Singing Boys*[92] as well as the more familiar *Five Hundred Points of Good Husbandry.*

In this case we can date with a fair amount of certainty Johnson's first acquaintance. Judging by the evidence of the *Dictionary,* Johnson did not begin to read Tusser (at least to take an interest in him) until some time after he began that herculean work.[93] The further he progressed, the more frequently he quoted

[89] Warton, *Observations on the Faerie Queene,* pp. 246-7 (reference to Gascoigne); pp. 268-70 (long note with account of his work); pp. 269-70 (mention of his critical discourse).

[90] Johnson, *Life of Dryden, Lives,* II, 184.

[91] Thirty-seven times in the first six letters of the alphabet.

[92] Quotation under *breast.*

[93] In the first edition of the *Dictionary* there is no quotation from Tusser under A, B, and C, and only one under D.

from Tusser;[94] and the numerous new quotations he added in 1773 show clearly that his interest did not lapse after twenty years.

It is hard to explain exactly why Tusser should have appealed so strongly to him. He had a lifelong interest in husbandry and quotes frequently in the *Dictionary* from Mortimer's *Husbandry*. For a town-bred man, he had a remarkable knowledge of and liking for things rural—tenantry, agriculture, thatching, cattle breeding. He had a great respect for proprietors of land and often amused himself with imaginary schemes of what he would do if he owned a country estate or an arable island. Tusser's homely good sense and unpretentiousness probably appealed to him, too. There are few English poets, apart from those of the first rank, of whom Johnson's knowledge can be so definitely determined.

Although it does not, strictly speaking, concern us here, it may be remarked that Johnson was fairly well acquainted with the scholars and prose writers of this period. He knew of the work of Linacer, Cheke, Gardiner and Haddon in furthering the study of the classics.[95] He had read Latimer's sermons, and quotes from them in the *Dictionary*[96] and also in his notes on Shakespeare.[97] He was familiar with that storehouse of the Elizabethan dramatists, Painter's *Palace of Pleasure*.[98] He speaks of Wilson as 'a man celebrated for the politeness of his style, and the extent of his knowledge,' and quotes a lengthy paragraph from the *Art of Rhetoricke*.[99]

In 1763 he had written a brief life of Ascham, prefixed to an edition of Ascham's English works of which Johnson was probably the editor;[100] and his frequent quotations in the *Dictionary*, both from *Toxophilus* and the *Schoolmaster*,[101] show the extent

---

[94] In the first edition :   A—0; B—0; C—0; D—1; E—3; F—24.
    In the revised: A—1; B—1; C—5; D—2; E—3; F—25.
[95] Johnson, Preface, *Shakespeare*, 1765, I, xxxii.
[96] Under *contrary* and *estate*. *Latimer's Sermons* is Item 628, p. 27, in the *Catalogue* of Johnson's library.
[97] Johnson, *Shakespeare*, 1765, I, 208; II, 514.
[98] *ibid.*, I, 338; III, 32.
[99] Introduction to the *Dictionary*.
[100] Boswell, *Life*, I, 537, note 2.
[101] Twelve times under the letter F.

of his knowledge of those two works. He mentions Ascham frequently in his notes on Shakespeare,[102] and again, in his *Life of Milton* he speaks of Ascham and criticizes his Latin verse.[103]

Thus we see that Johnson's knowledge of English poetry, as well as prose, before 1579 was not inconsiderable; and since this portion of English literature really fell outside his scheme for the *Dictionary*, which is by far the most fruitful field for investigation of his knowledge of early literature, it is remarkable that we have definite evidence that he knew so much. The main body of quotations in the *Dictionary* Johnson drew from writers of the period 1579-1660, believing that they are the 'wells of English undefiled, the pure sources of genuine diction.'[104] To supplement, and give some idea of the development of the language and literature culminating in this golden period, he wrote, as an introduction, his *History of the English Language,* which is, of necessity, brief. If space had permitted, or if Johnson had revised his Introduction in 1773, he might have included some of the poets he had, perforce, to pass over in silence.

[102] Johnson, *Shakespeare,* 1765, I, 136; I, 386; II, 77-8.
[103] Johnson, *Lives,* I, 123.
[104] Preface to the *Dictionary.*

IV

SPENSER TO THE RESTORATION

1579-1660

JOHNSON was a better Elizabethan scholar than he is generally given credit for being. He approached Elizabethan literature in the proper spirit. In 1754 he wrote to Thomas Warton: 'You have shewn to all, who shall hereafter attempt the study of our ancient authours, the way to success; by directing them to the perusal of the books which those authours had read. . . . The reason why the authours, which are yet read, of the sixteenth century, are so little understood, is, that they are read alone; and no help is borrowed from those who lived with them, or before them.'[1]

Eighteenth century scholars and critics were busy reclaiming the works of the minor Elizabethans. Their prime motive was to discover Shakespeare's sources and to throw more light on Shakespearean usage. In the course of these investigations, however, many Elizabethan writers were rediscovered and read for their own sakes. Gerard Langbaine had begun examining Shakespeare's sources in his *Account of the English Dramatick Poets* (1691). Rowe, Pope, Theobald, and subsequent editors continued the work. Johnson himself made no original contributions,[2] but he was an enthusiastic furtherer of these investigations, in which several of his friends were engaged. He wrote the Preface to Mrs. Lennox's *Shakespeare Illustrated* (1753). He encouraged Warton and was one of the first to praise Dr. Farmer's discoveries.[3] Through these friends he came to know of several of the minor sixteenth century writers from whose works Shakespeare took the plots of his plays.

Practically all of the greatest Elizabethans Johnson knew thoroughly—Sidney, Spenser, Shakespeare, Jonson; and, among

---

[1] Boswell, *Life*, I, 314. See also Raleigh, *Johnson on Shakespeare*, p. 167.

[2] For an explanation of his attribution of Shakespeare's source of *As You Like It* to 'a little pamphlet of those times,' see Nichol Smith, *Shakespeare in the Eighteenth Century*, p. 51.

[3] Boswell, *Life*, III, 45 and note 1; II, 131.

prose writers Hooker, Sidney, Raleigh, Knolles, and Bacon. The only really considerable name lacking is that of Marlowe, whom he seems to have known hardly at all. He had some knowledge of such men as Holinshed, Lodge, Robert Greene,[4] Thomas North, and John Lily.[5] He knew Webbe's *Discourse of English Poetrie* and Puttenham's *Art of English Poetrie.*[6] He was even acquainted with that curious work, Verstegen's *Restitution of Decayed Intelligence,*[7] and very familiar with Camden.[8] Of the lesser poets he knew Sir John Davies, Raleigh, Drayton, Daniel, Chapman, Harington, Sylvester, and Hall.

Bacon, Raleigh, and Hooker were especial favorites of Johnson's. They figure prominently among his sources of a speech 'adéquate to all the purposes of use and elegance'—Bacon for terms of natural knowledge; Raleigh for the phrases of policy, war, and navigation; Hooker for the language of theology.[9] From the works of all three he quotes extensively in the *Dictionary,*[10] and all three he continued to read throughout his life. In his *Life of Waller* he points out a plagiarism from Hooker,[11] which is proof of the soundness of his knowledge; and in the 122nd number of the *Rambler,* an interesting discussion of early English historians, he pays tribute both to Knolles and to Raleigh.[12]

Of the three, however, he had the highest praise for Bacon, whom he had never read until he began compiling his *Dictionary.*[13] He made up for it by reading Bacon continuously until the end of his life. His works are filled with quotations and axioms from Bacon—the *Essays, Advancement of Learning, History of Henry*

[4] Johnson, *Shakespeare,* 1773, I, 199: '... Green, one of the first among us who made a trade of writing pamphlets, published *A Detection of the Frauds and Tricks of Coney-Catchers* and Couzeners.'

[5] Lily's *Grammar Construed* is quoted under *dodkin* in the *Dictionary.* Another reference to Lily—Johnson, *Shakespeare,* 1765, I, xxxii. Lily's *Cupid and Campaspe* song is quoted in Percy's *Reliques,* III, 86.

[6] Johnson, *Lives,* II, 103.

[7] Quoted under *crone.*

[8] See Appendix.

[9] Preface to the *Dictionary.*

[10] Under the letters E and F: from Raleigh 87 times; from Hooker 239 times; from Bacon 476 times.

[11] Johnson, *Lives,* I, 339-40.

[12] Johnson, *Works,* V, 330-1. Knolles, of course, was responsible for the plot of *Irene.*

[13] Boswell, *Life,* III, 220.

VII, Wisdom of the Ancients, and *Physical Remains.*[14] He remarked to Seward that a dictionary of the English language
might be compiled from Bacon's writings alone; and he at one
time contemplated an edition of Bacon's English works, together
with a biography.[15]

Johnson's knowledge of Elizabethan and early Jacobean prose
was excellent for his time, his knowledge of the non-dramatic
poetry fairly good; but his knowledge of the drama, while remarkably complete in a few instances, was confined to only four
playwrights.

II

Johnson knew little or nothing about the origins of English
drama, or about pre-Shakespearean plays. He may have glanced
through Percy's essay *On the Origin of the English Stage;*[16] and
he had read the various notes of Theobald, Warburton,[17] and Steevens on the subject. But this, apart from whatever information he
may have got from Oldys, Warton, and Farmer, was all he knew
about the old Miracle plays, Moralities, and Interludes. He quotes
in his *Shakespeare* the notes of preceding editors, often with a
sly dig at their ingenuity; but the only contribution he offers
himself is the suggestion that 'the *Vice* of the old farce, to whom
Punch succeeds, used to fight the devil with a wooden dagger.'[18]
He refers to *Gorboduc,* as we have seen, and to Kyd's *Hieronymo;*[19] but it is most probable that his information was second-
hand—gleaned from the notes and quotations of Theobald and
Warburton.[20] On the famous Falstaffian burlesque scene in *Henry
IV—Part I* he has one interesting note, which seems to imply
that he had dipped into Thomas Preston's *Cambyses:* 'I question
if *Shakespeare* had ever seen this tragedy; for there is a remark-

---

[14] Johnson, *Ramblers No. 106* and *137, Works,* V, 226, 420; Johnson, *Idlers No.
27* and *92, Works,* VII, 107, 371; Johnson, *Shakespeare,* 1765, II, 355, etc.

[15] Boswell, *Life,* III, 220-1.

[16] Percy, *Reliques,* I, 118-28, an account of early drama, mentioning *Everyman,
Hick-Scorner, Gorboduc, Jocasta,* and the *Supposes.*

[17] He quotes a long note of Warburton's on Miracles and Moralities in his
Shakespeare, 1765, V, 362-5.

[18] *ibid.,* IV, 455; also II, 431.

[19] Preface to *Shakespeare,* 1765, I, xliii.

[20] Johnson quotes a full note on Kyd by Theobald in his *Shakespeare,* 1765, III,
4; see also VI, 364.

able peculiarity of measure, which, when he professed to speak in *King* Cambyses' *vein,* he would hardly have missed, if he had known it.'[21]

As for the plays of Peele, Lily, Greene, and Marlowe, it is impossible to discover whether he knew any of them.[22] That he had some general acquaintance with them is borne out by the low opinion of their merits he expresses: 'This however is certain, that he [Shakespeare] is the first who taught either tragedy or comedy to please, there being no theatrical piece of any older writer, of which the name is known, except to antiquaries and collectors of books, which are sought because they are scarce, and would not have been scarce, had they been much esteemed.'[23]

There is in this comment a trace of belligerence which one finds frequently in Johnson's criticism, and which causes one to cast about for the cause. It may be that someone in an unguarded moment had spoken extravagantly of these minor dramatists in Johnson's presence. More probably, in his editorial labors on Shakespeare, he had wearied of the long and tedious notes of Theobald and Warburton, citing obscure early plays for possible parallels—the parade of learning. Dodsley's famous *Collection of Old Plays* had been published in 1744, and it was a popular edition. Though he does not mention it, Johnson must surely have known of it. Six years before, Thomas Hayward in his *British Muse* had quoted from such plays as *Lust's Dominion,* the *Fair Quarrel,* the *Spanish Tragedy,* the *Merry Devil of Edmonton,* and from the plays of Lily, Marston, Dekker, Webster, Ford, Heywood, Tourneur, and Massinger. Also, in 1752 had appeared an interesting little book by William Chetwood, the *British Theatre,* a collection of brief lives of English poets and playwrights, including John Heywood, Thomas Preston, Sackville, Gascoigne, Marlowe, Kyd, Greene, Dekker, Lily, Middleton, Marston, Field, Webster, Tourneur, Ford, and others.

Johnson was overstating. The reader of the middle eighteenth century may have known many of the minor Elizabethan dramatists, at least by name. But he was right to the extent that, in

21 Johnson, *Shakespeare,* 1765, IV, 166.

22 Item 630, p. 27, in the *Catalogue* of his library is: 'A bundle of plays.' Unfortunately, no further description is given.

23 Johnson, *Shakespeare,* 1765, I, xliii; also I, xxxix.

general, the Englishmen of his age knew and read little Elizabethan drama other than Shakespeare, Jonson, Beaumont and
Fletcher.

Johnson's only reference to Marlowe is in connection with
one of his minor poems.[24] He may have known about Marlowe's
plays, but if so he took not the slightest interest in them. *Doctor
Faustus* and *Tamburlaine* were acted well into the seventeenth
century, but only in garbled form; and Marlowe's name soon
became synonymous with ranting, with burlesquings of 'the pam-
pered jades of Asia.' Dryden, in his discussions of the Elizabethans, even in the famous passage in *An Essay of Dramatic
Poesy*, never once refers to Marlowe. His plays were known, if
at all, only in an unrecognizably debased form such as the travesty
in twenty-six pages by the actor, Mountford, called the *Life and
Death of Doctor Faustus, made into a Farce*.[25] During the latter
part of the seventeenth century Shakespeare was often treated in
this manner, too;[26] but, unlike Marlowe, Shakespeare held his own
Knowledge of him was certainly far from being confined to such
burlesques. Johnson, then, cannot be blamed for being ignorant
of Marlowe. To know Marlowe in the eighteenth century was
to be a rare exception.

There is no need here to discuss Johnson's knowledge of
Shakespeare.[27] The value of his edition of Shakespeare and his
own merits as an editor have already been sufficiently considered
and properly estimated.[28] Johnson's *Proposals for an Edition of
Shakespeare's Works* and the Preface to the first edition of 1765

[24] For his quotations from the *Passionate Shepherd,* see pp. 70-2, below.

[25] *The Life and Death of Doctor Faustus, made into a Farce*—By Mr. Mountford. With the Humours of Harlequin and Scaramouche. London 1697. (Undoubtedly a travesty of Marlowe's play. There are many verses of his, as well as
echoes and a pitiful hodgepodge of Faustus' last soliloquy.)

[26] *The Wits, or, Sport upon Sport*. Being a Curious Collection of several Drolls
and Farces . . . Written I know not when, by several Persons, I know not who;
But now newly Collected by your Old Friend to please you, Francis Kirkman.
London, 1673. (This volume contains *Venus and Adonis, Bottom the Weaver,*
the *Bouncing Knight* [Falstaff], etc.)

[27] The First Folio of 1623 is Item 467, p. 21; the 1664 folio, Item 353, p. 17, in
the *Catalogue* of Johnson's library.

[28] By Sir Walter Raleigh in his Introduction to *Johnson on Shakespeare*; by
Professor Nichol Smith in *Shakespeare in the 18th Century*, and *Eighteenth Century Essays on Shakespeare* (1903).

have a secure and important place in the great body of Shake-spearean criticism. That he knew Shakespeare and knew him almost by heart no one who is acquainted with his various writ-ings can doubt. He quoted Shakespeare ceaselessly and appositely, both in his work and in his daily life, as Boswell is witness. He had, of course, his favorites, but in the *Dictionary,* where Shake-speare leads all others in number of quotations,[29] we find Johnson quoting from every single one of Shakespeare's plays. His opinion of Shakespeare, whom he loves 'this side idolatry as much as any,' is the touchstone of his literary criticism. Here we see him unbiased, outspoken; here is a clear statement of his critical position. Johnson's final estimate of Shakespeare is quite as fine in its way as that of the Coleridge school. There is in it always a wholesome sanity, which is sometimes missing in the romantic's evangelicalism. In this essay, however, we are more concerned with the sonnets and non-dramatic poems; and Johnson's knowl-edge of those we shall consider later.

Ben Jonson he knew well, but in a curiously limited way, seem-ingly.[30] To say that he was ignorant of Jonson's great trilogy would be unjustified; but he seems to have preferred and known best only a few of Jonson's plays—*Catiline, Sejanus, Every Man in his Humour,* and, strangely enough, the *New Inn.*[31] Judging from the assigned quotations in the *Dictionary,* his favorite was *Catiline.* He knew Jonson's prose and his non-dramatic verse far better than his plays. He quotes frequently from *Timber,*[32] and even more frequently from the lyrics in his masques and in collec-

---

[29] Shakespeare is quoted 699 times under A alone.

[30] '5 vols. of Ben Jonson's works' (no date)—Item 123, p. 8, *Catalogue* of Johnson's library.

[31] Under C, D, E, Jonson's poetry is quoted seventy-four times. Unfortunately, Johnson does not often give more than the name of the author. To find the context of all these quotations would be unprofitable. I give a few:

Tavern Academy: caterer, drawer.
Catiline: cobswan, come, condition, disgracefully, dormouse, double, emulate.
Epigrams: cony.
Forest: court.
Underwoods: cut and long tail, emissary.
Discoveries: flag, fruitfulness.
Everyman in his Humour: Bedstaff.
New Inn: fleshquake, knit.

[32] Thirteen times under E and F.

tions like *Underwoods*; but owing to Jonson's close association with Jacobean poetry, it may be well to postpone for the moment a consideration of the extent of Johnson's knowledge of his non-dramatic verse.

Beaumont and Fletcher share Dryden's praise with Shakespeare and Jonson; and these were the four great Elizabethan dramatists to the eighteenth century as well as to Dryden's age. One would expect Johnson to know Beaumont and Fletcher fairly well; most of the educated men of his time did—far better than we know them today. Jonson's works appeared in a new edition in 1716, and an edition of the plays of Beaumont and Fletcher had been brought out five years before. But though Johnson knew a later editor of Beaumont and Fletcher, Mr. Seward,[33] very well, he does not appear to have cared for Beaumont and Fletcher, nor to have known very much about them, except from hearsay. In the first edition of the *Dictionary* he quotes from their collaboration the *Scornful Lady* once,[34] and twice from Fletcher's *Queen of Corinth*.[35] In the revised edition of 1773 he adds one more quotation—from *Dioclesian*.[36]

Of all the plays of Beaumont and Fletcher it seems surprising that he should have chosen to quote from those particular ones. The explanation is simple. While at work on the *Dictionary,* for quotations from Shakespeare he used Warburton's edition, which came out about that time (1747);[37] and in glancing through Warburton's notes he came across one or two quotations containing the word he was illustrating from Shakespeare and casually included them along with the Shakespearean illustrations he was quoting. Every single quotation from Beaumont and Fletcher in the first edition of the *Dictionary* Johnson simply transcribed from the notes in Warburton's *Shakespeare*.[38] We can readily

[33] Johnson, *Shakespeare*, 1765, VI, 408: 'A skein of silk is called a *sleeve* of silk, as I learned from Mr. *Seward,* the ingenious editor of *Beaumont* and *Fletcher.*'

[34] Under *gord.*

[35] Under *circle* and *starch.*

[36] Under *brewis.* This quotation, in all probability, Johnson found in Steevens' notes to the revised *Shakespeare* of 1773; but I did not succeed in finding it.

[37] 'Warburton's Shakespeare, 8 v.'—Item 131. p. 8, *Catalogue* of Johnson's library.

[38] See Appendix.

understand why he quotes so seldom from Beaumont and Fletcher and why his choice in those few instances seems strange. He possibly knew no play of theirs at first hand.[39]

Apart from these four, Johnson quotes no other Elizabethan dramatist in the *Dictionary*, with the exception of two surprising additions in 1773. Under *poking-stick,* a word not included in the first edition, he quotes two verses from Middleton's *Blurt Master Constable*; and under *rabato* (also not included in the first edition) two verses from an 'Old Comedy.'[40] The way in which he gives the attribution of the former is unusual: 'Middleton's Blurt Master Constable, a Comedy, 1602.' It is the only instance in which he gives the date of any work from which he is quoting. One is inclined at first to think that some one of his friends had lent him a rare old volume, and that when he quoted from it he looked at the title-page and copied down date and all.

For additional quotations from Shakespeare in the revised edition of the *Dictionary,* instead of using Warburton again, Johnson naturally used the new edition of his own *Shakespeare,* with which George Steevens was helping him. And just as in the former instance, he included these two quotations from notes on Shakespeare supplied this time by George Steevens.[41] *Blurt Master Constable* was a favorite of Steevens'; he quotes from it eight times in his notes, and on every occasion gives the title with date, just as Johnson gives it in the *Dictionary*.

Of the plays of Webster, Ford, Tourneur, Massinger, and the rest of the lesser Elizabethan dramatists it is safe to say that Johnson knew practically nothing, except, perhaps, their names and the few scattered verses quoted by Theobald, Warburton, and Steevens in their notes. Chapman was one of his favorite poets, as we shall see; yet it is extremely doubtful that he knew Chapman's plays. Johnson did not care particularly for drama as drama.[42] He admired Shakespeare and delighted in his works.

[39] Item 612, p. 27, in the *Catalogue* of Johnson's library, however, is 'Beaumont and Fletcher's plays, 10 v. 1750.'
[40] The 'Old Comedy' is the *Comedy of Law Trickes,* 1608.
[41] See Appendix.
[42] Tinker, *Dr. Johnson and Fanny Burney,* p. 110: 'He [Johnson] laughed, but told me repeatedly (I mean twice, which, for him, is very remarkable) that I might depend upon all the service in his power; and, he added, it would be well

To a lesser degree he admired a few other dramatists, and even tried his hand at playwrighting once himself. But, while there is no doubt that he considered Shakespeare the glory of English literature, he did not necessarily consider Elizabethan drama the glory of the Elizabethan age.

III

Except for authorities who have made him a special study, few men have known Spenser more thoroughly than Johnson. He read and reread his Spenser—prose[43] as well as verse. Johnson quotes from his poetry throughout the whole of the *Dictionary*,[44] and these quotations cover the whole range of Spenser's work— *Muipotmos, Tears of the Muses, Mother Hubbard's Tale,* the *Epithalamion, Prothalamion,* and *Four Hymns,* as well as the *Faerie Queene, Shepherd's Calendar* and *Amoretti.* As with Shakespeare and Bacon, Johnson's works are studded with quotations from Spenser and comments on his work. Numbers 36, 37, and 121 of the *Rambler* are devoted to a discussion of Spenser and the pastoral. If all of these scattered remarks are collected they will be found to make up a substantial body of Spenserian criticism.[44a]

Johnson once confided to Boswell that he would willingly have undertaken a *Life of Spenser* if he had been able to obtain any new material;[45] but new material for the life of Spenser has always been difficult to find and still is for the modern biographer.

---

to make Murphy the last judge, "for he knows the stage," he said, "and I am quite ignorant of it." ' See also Hawkins, *Life,* pp. 440-1, for an interesting account of Johnson's attitude toward his editing of Shakespeare.

[43] Johnson quotes, under the letters E and F in the *Dictionary,* sixty-four times from Spenser's *State of Ireland.*

[44] One hundred forty-five times under A; one hundred sixty-four times under C, etc.

   Pastorals: abacke, aligge, appay, carve, cock, cockle, etc.

   Faerie Queene: passim.

   Hubbard's Tale: abate, afterclap, awhape, aworking, chafe, etc.

   Epithalamion: all, carol, ceremonies, count, crowd, etc.

   Sonnets: assuagement.

   Tears of the Muses: cherishment.

   Muipotmos: covertly.

[44a] They have been collected in J. E. Brown's valuable *Critical Opinions of Samuel Johnson,* Princeton, 1926.

[45] Boswell, *Life,* IV, 473; II, 48, note 2.

Johnson, as his guarded comments on Hughes' edition (1715)[46] show, was not a Spenserian scholar and made no claim to being one; but he knew Spenser's poetry thoroughly, and he appreciated fully the extent of Spenser's innovations. As we have already seen, he encouraged—even prodded on—the somewhat lethargic Warton to finish his *Observations on the Faerie Queene*,[47] a book which he must have read with eagerness when it appeared in 1754.

Johnson was by no means ignorant of the forces which shaped Spenser's poetry and spurred him to achieve for England what had been achieved for Italy and France. Being a sound classical scholar, he knew Spenser's indebtedness to Virgil and Mantuan and understood the full significance of the *Shepherd's Calendar*.[48] He appreciated, too, the ideals and aspirations of the age. He shared Spenser's and Sidney's admiration for Castiglione's *Courtier,* a book which he knew very well indeed.[49] He certainly looked upon Spenser as having succeeded in giving England a great poetry comparable, if not superior, to that of the Italian and French Renascence. He wrote, as admitting no doubt, 'We consider the whole succession from *Spenser* to *Pope* as superior to any names which the continent can boast.'[50]

He admired and read most the *Faerie Queene;* but he was also very fond of quoting from *Mother Hubbard's Tale,* and he preferred the *Epithalamion* to the *Prothalamion.* Despite his limited ear, he appreciated the Spenserian stanza, its advantages and difficulties.[51] But the Spenserian stanza in the hands of its skilful inventor is quite another thing from the same difficult stanza in the hands of a lesser poet. There is a deal of good sense in Johnson's caution to the horde of Spenserian imitators. He heartily endorses Spenser's fictions and sentiments, but warns

[46] It is impossible to prove definitely which edition of Spenser Johnson used. He certainly knew Hughes' edition, and probably earlier ones as well. See Johnson, *Life of Hughes, Lives,* II, 425-6.

[47] Boswell, *Life,* I, 321, 323, 335.

[48] See numbers of the *Rambler* mentioned above. Also Johnson, *Life of A. Philips, Lives,* IV, 290-3.

[49] There was a new edition of the *Courtier* in 1727. References: Johnson, *Life of Addison, Lives,* II, 337; Johnson, *Rambler No. 208, Works,* VI, 393; Johnson, *Shakespeare,* 1765, II, 181; Boswell, *Journal,* V, 314. Item 403, p. 19, in the *Catalogue* of Johnson's library is a copy of the *Courtier.*

[50] Johnson, *Idler No. 91, Works,* VII, 366.

[51] Johnson, *Life of Prior, Lives,* III, 38-9.

against attempts to copy the stanza and diction.[52] He was of his great predecessor's mind, that 'Spenser, in imitating the ancients, writ no language.' He would have been false to himself had he not censured Spenser's diction. His criticism, however, is directed not so much at the *Faerie Queene* as at the more extreme and youthful *Shepherd's Calendar,* of which he says quite sensibly, 'Surely, at the same time that a shepherd learns theology, he may gain some acquaintance with his native language.'[53] Spenser himself greatly modified his diction before writing his masterpiece.

On most of these occasions Johnson has in mind the eighteenth century imitators of Spenser. His stand in the matter is a very sound one. He felt that Spenser had evolved for himself a type of poetry which was open to criticism in some respects. The fact that Spenser himself had succeeded through sheer genius in making it great poetry (and there can be no doubt of Johnson's opinion about that) seemed to him no proof that others could do the same or should attempt it. His occasionally harsh criticism of the pastoral is very largely owing to his exasperation at the 'numbers without number' who had attempted pastorals in imitation of Spenser.[54] This exasperation colors his notorious censure of *Lycidas.* If we glance through the mass of uninspired pastoral verse of the eighteenth century, we can sympathize to some extent with Johnson. He knew, too, other seventeenth century pastorals than Milton's—'. . . there had never, from the time of Spenser, wanted writers to talk occasionally of *Arcadia* and *Strephon.*'[55] He certainly knew Phineas Fletcher's *Piscatory Eclogues.* Though he does not mention Fletcher in his discussion of Sannazarius and the shortcomings of the piscatory type of eclogue,[56] that was probably owing to the fact that he did not come across Fletcher's eclogues until shortly after this number of the *Rambler* was written.[57] Despite his strictures on the pastoral and on the *Shep-*

[52] Johnson, *Rambler No. 121, Works,* V, 326.

[53] Johnson, *Rambler No. 37, Works,* IV, 242. He is referring here, specifically, to the *September Eclogue.*

[54] Johnson, *Life of West, Lives,* IV, 307.

[55] Johnson, *Life of Philips, Lives,* IV, 292.

[56] Johnson, *Rambler No. 36, Works,* IV, 236-7.

[57] The *Rambler* began coming out in 1750, while Johnson was just beginning his work on the *Dictionary.* He quotes Fletcher only once (six lines under *foreslow*), in the first as well as the revised edition.

herd's Calendar, he quotes from it frequently in the *Dictionary,* as we have already seen.

That he was not bigoted on the subject of the pastoral is shown by his fondness for Sidney's *Arcadia,*[58] a book which remained popular well into the eighteenth century and was finally supplanted only by the novel. Johnson was well aware that Shakespeare had borrowed the idea of the scene between Gloucester and Edgar (*Lear,* Act IV, scene vi) from Sidney.[59] For Sidney's poetry he seems to have cared less, though he quotes from it with fair frequency in the *Dictionary,*[60] and he associates Sidney with Spenser as the source of the purest 'dialect of poetry and fiction.'[61] Usually the verses he quotes are from the pastoral and classical metre poems scattered throughout the *Arcadia;*[62] but he quotes occasionally from *Astrophel and Stella.*[63]

Johnson knew, then, two of the three greatest sonnet sequences of Elizabethan poetry, Sidney's and Spenser's; but, strangely enough, he does not appear to have known the third—Shakespeare's. Of all the eighteenth century editors of Shakespeare, Malone was the first to depart from the tradition begun by Heming and Condel and include the sonnets (1790). George Steevens had refused to print them in the new edition of Johnson's *Shakespeare* entrusted to him.[64] The eighteenth century, however, had means of knowing some of Shakespeare's nondramatic poems. Early in the century Lintot had published (no date) what purported to be a reprint of a collection of the minor poems originally 'printed for W. Jaggard, 1599.' This interesting little volume, which looks almost as if it were made up from publisher's remainders (each section has a separate title-page), contains *Venus and Adonis,* the *Rape of Lucrece,* the *Passionate Pilgrim,* and *Sonnets to Sundry Notes of Musicke;* but it does not include the sonnets.[65] Mrs. Cooper overlooks the sonnets in

[58] Quoted one hundred twenty-one times under the letters E and F.

[59] Johnson, *Shakespeare,* 1765, VI, 122.

[60] Fifty-four times under A, B, C, D, E.

[61] Preface to the *Dictionary.*

[62] Quoted under *ability, after-liver, cabin,* etc.

[63] Quoted under *spright, stammer,* etc.

[64] Nichol Smith, *Shakespeare in the 18th Century,* p. 57.

[65] In the advertisement in front of this little volume Lintot refers to 'a late Edition of his Dramatick Works in Six Volumes. . . . I shall not take upon me to

her *Muses Library,* but gives thirteen stanzas from the *Rape of Lucrece* and mentions *Venus and Adonis.*[66] Winstanley and Phillips[67] fail to mention the sonnets; but both mention *Venus* and *Lucrece,* and Winstanley quotes two stanzas from the former.[68]

As for the sonnets, there can be no doubt that they were generally neglected until Malone printed them in his edition six years after Johnson's death. It is quite improbable that Johnson had any knowledge of them at all.[69] But *Venus and Adonis* and the *Rape of Lucrece* he had several opportunities of reading. Both Warburton and Theobald knew these poems well, and Johnson quotes several of their notes on Shakespeare referring to *Venus and Lucrece.*[70] He himself quotes from the latter at least once in his *Dictionary,*[71] but in this instance he is not quoting from the poem itself, but from a note of Theobald's which Warburton prints in his edition of Shakespeare, the edition Johnson was reading at the time.[72] It is impossible to secure all the evidence, but it is probable that Johnson's knowledge of these two poems of Shakespeare's consisted only of what he learned from the notes of Theobald and Warburton.

There is a rather puzzling mistaken attribution to Shakespeare in his *Dictionary,* which is interesting in this connection. In the first edition, under *youth,* he quotes four lines from Raleigh's *Nymph's Reply,* attributing them to Shakespeare. Warburton is again at least partly responsible. In his notes on the *Merry Wives of Windsor,* in which Sir Hugh quotes two lines from the *Passionate Shepherd to his Love,* Warburton writes: 'This is part

say anything of the Author, an ingenious Person having compil'd some Memoirs of his Life, and prefix'd it to the late above mention'd Edition.' This is certainly Rowe's edition, which came out in 1709. Therefore the date of Lintot's undated *Collection* is probably 1710. 'Shakespeare's *Poems,* 1710' is in the *Catalogue* of the Warton library—Item 10389, p. 316. This must be a copy of Lintot.

[66] Mrs. Cooper, *Muses Library,* pp. 376-80.

[67] Philips, *Theatrum Poetarum,* p. 194 (Modern Writers section).

[68] Winstanley, *Lives,* p. 131.

[69] The hundreds of undesignated quotations from Shakespeare in the *Dictionary,* however, would have to be verified before Johnson's ignorance could be incontrovertibly proved.

[70] Johnson, *Shakespeare,* 1765, I, 189; VI, 405-6 (quotes seven lines), 608 (quotes five lines) ; VII, 267—from Warburton. *ibid.,* II, 59—from Theobald.

[71] Under *cloth* Johnson quotes two lines from *Tarquin and Lucrece.* In the revised edition the lines are marked 'Shakespeare.'

[72] Warburton, *Shakespeare,* II, 341.

of a beautiful little poem of the author's, which poem, and the answer to it, the reader will not be displeased to find here.'[73] He then proceeds to quote both poems in full. Just before and just after the quotation from the *Nymph's Reply* in the first edition of the *Dictionary* are two quotations from Shakespeare. Johnson must have been searching through Warburton's edition for illustrations from Shakespeare, happened to notice these poems, which he had read before,[74] in the notes, and inserted the two lines, carelessly accepting Warburton's attribution of authorship. When he came to revise the *Dictionary* in 1773, he corrected the error; his own edition of Shakespeare shows that he had discovered it before 1765.

This is only one instance in Johnson's curious relationship with these two companion poems. Both were evidently great favorites of his. He quotes from them seven times[75] in the *Dictionary*—at least once possibly from memory;[76] yet in every case (except the instance mentioned above, which was subsequently corrected) he gives Raleigh as the author. As we have already seen, Johnson was quoting from Warburton's notes the lines under *youth,* and Warburton's attribution is to Shakespeare. Why, then, the attribution in all but one instance to Raleigh?

Isaak Walton had reprinted both songs in his *Compleat Angler,* attributing them correctly to Marlowe and Raleigh. Percy, who quotes the *Passionate Shepherd to his Love* in the *Reliques,* goes into the whole matter of authorship and concludes that this poem is certainly Marlowe's, and the *Reply* Raleigh's. Johnson knew Walton very well.[77] He knew the *Reliques,* too; but that book, of course, was not published until ten years after the first appearance of the *Dictionary.* The explanation of the attributions to Raleigh may be only a confused memory of Walton. But when

[73] Warburton, *Shakespeare,* I, 294-5.

[74] In the *Gentlemen's Magazine.* See p. 72, below.

[75] Under *field* (P.S.), *fold* (N.R.), *ivy* (P.S.), *kirtle* (N.R.), *slipper* (P.S.), *valley* (P.S.), *youth* (N.R.)—all in the first and fourth editions.

[76] Under *valley* Johnson misquotes the first stanza of the *Passionate Shepherd* (correctly quoted under *field*), confusing the third and fourth verses and giving them as one.

[77] He quotes Walton under *expire,* etc. See also Boswell, *Life,* II, 320, 326, 417—references to Walton's *Lives; ibid.,* IV, 360—reference to the *Compleat Angler.*

Johnson edited Shakespeare in 1765 he copied in his notes on the *Merry Wives of Windsor* Warburton's introductory statement about these two poems (see pp. 70-1 above), printed the poems just as Warburton did, adding the remark: 'These two Poems, which Dr. Warburton gives to Shakespeare, are, by writers nearer that time, disposed of, one to Marlowe, the other to Raleigh. These poems are read in different copies with great Variations.' Percy was at this time preparing his *Reliques* for publication, and it may have been he who put Johnson straight on the matter of authorship.

The last statement in Johnson's note quoted above is interesting. Although he was certainly writing his notes with Warburton open before him, although he copies verbatim Warburton's comment, he actually prints a different version of the two poems from that given by Warburton—different as well from that given by Percy.[78] He does not say where he came across his version, which is rare and includes an extra stanza; but his text of both poems is to be found in a letter to Mr. Urban, October 25, 1739, printed in the *Gentlemen's Magazine,* Volume IX.[79] The *Passionate Shepherd to his Love* is the only poem of Marlowe's, seemingly, that Johnson had read, and the comment quoted above is the single occasion of his ever referring to Marlowe in any way.

Raleigh was primarily a prose writer, and it was his prose that Johnson knew best; but he had read other poems of Raleigh's besides the *Nymph's Reply*. Apart from this poem, he quotes Raleigh's verse four times in the first edition of the *Dictionary,* and when he revised it added a fifth quotation.[80] In his *Life of Milton* he mentions a short poem in blank verse 'tending to reconcile the nation to Raleigh's wild attempt upon Guiana, and probably written by Raleigh himself.'[81] In 1750 he wrote to his friend, Dr. Birch, who was engaged on an edition of Raleigh's smaller pieces, enclosing a 'manuscript, which fell by chance within my

[78] Percy's version is substantially the same as that given by Walton. Warburton's version is that given in the 1640 edition of Shakespeare's *Poems,* from which he also secured the second stanza of *Take O Take those Lips Away* in a note on *Measure for Measure* (reprinted by Johnson, *Shakespeare,* 1765, I, 337). Lintot prints only four stanzas of the *Passionate Shepherd* and one of the *Nymph's Reply*.

[79] For this hint I am indebted to Professor Nichol Smith, *Warton's History of English Poetry*, p. 12.

[80] Quoted under *carouse, contrariwise, trust, wanton* in the first edition. Quotation under *cates* added in the fourth edition.   [81] Johnson, *Lives*, I, 259.

notice,' and which he believed to be in Raleigh's handwriting.[82]
What this manuscript was we shall probably never know. Boswell
knew nothing about it, except that he believed it to have belonged
to Mrs. Williams.

Johnson had not even a passing acquaintance with Raleigh's
and Sidney's friend, Fulke Greville, or with Giles Fletcher, Constable, Barnabe Barnes, Campion, and Robert Southwell; but he
knew Sir John Davies, Chapman, Drayton, Daniel, Harington,
and Hall—the first three very well indeed.

Of Hall, Daniel, and Sir John Harington his knowledge was
limited. He was familiar with Bishop Hall's prose;[83] but he never
quotes from his poems or mentions him as a poet but twice.
Under the word *satirist* in the revised, not the first, edition of the
Dictionary he quotes the familiar boast:

'I first adventure, follow me who list
And be the second English satirist.'

This quotation he might have come across anywhere. It only
shows, at the most, that he had looked into Hall's *Satires*.[84] His
only other quotation from Hall's poetry is two verses from the
Account of a Servile Tutor in his notes in the 1773 edition of his
Shakespeare.[85] There was a new edition of Hall's *Virgidemiarum,
Satires in Six Books* in 1753. If Johnson knew this edition, he
seems not to have learned of it until some years after its publication.

It was not until the revised edition of the *Dictionary* that
he quoted Sir John Harington, and then only once.[86] The lines
he quotes are one of the epigrams:

'I read the satire thou entitlest first,
And laid aside the rest, and overpast,
And swore I thought the writer was accurst,
That his first satire had not been his last.'

---

[82] Boswell, *Life*, I, 262-3. Birch, *Works of Sir Walter Ralegh, Kt*. London,
MDCCLI, II, 393-4, has a five-stanza version of the two poems discussed above,
differing from Johnson's, Warburton's and Percy's.

[83] Quoted four times under E and F (*ever, fatherhood, foreslow, forethink*) ;
three times under O and P (*obtrude, pardonableness, puddle*)'.

[84] See Johnson, *Life of Dryden, Lives*, II, 184, for a reference to Hall's satires
'published five years before the death of Elizabeth.'

[85] Johnson, *Shakespeare*, 1773, I, 290.　　　　[86] Under *overpass*.

There was a copy of Harington's *Epigrams* (1629) and a copy of the 1633 edition of his works in the Harleian Collection,[87] which Johnson may have glanced through. There was also a copy of the 1634 edition of *Orlando* and the *Epigrams* in the Wartons' library;[88] but the text of this epigram (Epigram No. 41, the First Book, Pp2) differs from that quoted by Johnson.[89] Mrs. Cooper used this 1634 edition when she reprinted this same epigram in her *Muses Library*; but there are strong reasons for believing that Johnson did not know the *Muses Library*.[90] It may be that he was quoting from memory; he knew Harington's verse better than he knew Hall's. In 1769 Dr. Harrington printed for the first time some miscellaneous poems and letters of his ancestor in *Nugae Antiquae*. This Johnson certainly knew; he called it a 'very pretty book,' and the year before his death he urged Dr. Harrington to publish another volume.[91] The epigram in question is not in *Nugae Antiquae*.

With Samuel Daniel he had more than a passing acquaintance,[92] but the only two works of Daniel's from which he quotes are the *Civil Wars* and *Musophilus*;[93] the former he read a second time, judging from the new quotations from that poem he adds in the revised edition of the *Dictionary*. Of this group of poets, however, his favorites were Chapman, Drayton, and Sir John Davies.

Johnson's knowledge of Sir John Davies' poetry is confined almost entirely[94] to one poem, *Nosce Teipsum*, but that he read and reread and greatly admired. His admiration for *Nosce Teipsum* began before 1750[95] and lasted until his death. He read Davies in Nahum Tate's edition, which was first published in

[87] *Harleian Catalogue*, IV, 644; III, 238.

[88] *A Catalogue of Books*, p. 31, Item 860.

[89] This epigram does not occur in the 1613 or 1615 editions of Harington's epigrams.

[90] See Appendix.

[91] Boswell, *Life*, IV, 207. See also Johnson, *Shakespeare*, 1765, VI, 575.

[92] He quotes from Daniel under A, B, C, D, E, twenty-seven times.

[93] He quotes from *Musophilus* under *viperous* and *unafflicted*.

[94] In the Appendix to Volume II, *Shakespeare*, 1773, X, Johnson remarks: 'John Davies begins one of his epigrams upon proverbs:

"He sets cocke *on* the hoope, *in*, you would say;
For cocking *in hoopes* is now all the play." '

[95] Davies is quoted extensively in the first edition of the *Dictionary*—fifty-two times under the first three letters of the alphabet.

1697, reprinted in 1714, and again in 1715.[96] Owing to the fact
that the second and third editions are close reprints of the first,
it is impossible to determine which Johnson used. It is probable,
however, that he used the first edition of 1697, which he may
have bought from Osborne at the Harleian sale.

Johnson's quotations from Davies are not limited to the *Dictionary*. He quotes a stanza from *Nosce Teipsum* in his *Life of
Sir Thomas Browne* (1756)[97] and ten lines in his notes on the
Comedy of Errors.[98] In his *Life of Waller* he voices his admiration for Davies: 'He might have studied with advantage the
poem of Davis, which, though merely philosophical, yet seldom
leaves the ear ungratified.'[99] He had also read Davies' *Defence of
Ireland*;[100] this, too, he may have bought at Osborne's sale.[101]

Chapman's poetry he likewise knew only in part. He does not
appear to have read either the plays or Chapman's continuation
of *Hero and Leander*—or, in fact, anything of Chapman's save
his two verse translations, the *Iliad* and the *Odyssey*. In the *Dictionary* he quotes from these two poems with more and more
frequency the further he proceeds.[102] He preferred the *Iliad* to the
Odyssey. That he continued to read Chapman's Homer is shown
by new additions added in the revised *Dictionary*[103] and by the
frequency with which he mentions Chapman and illustrates from
his translations in the *Lives of the Poets*.[104] He remarks that
Chapman, very popular until the end of the seventeenth century,
was in the eighteenth almost totally neglected. As a translator of
Homer he had been superseded by Pope—a fact which makes
Johnson's devotion to Chapman all the more remarkable.

[96] Johnson did not use Mrs. Cooper's selections in the *Muses Library,* or
Capell's reprint in *Prolusions,* which was not published until five years after the
first appearance of the *Dictionary.* See Appendix.

[97] Johnson, *Works,* XII, 304.

[98] Johnson, *Shakespeare,* 1765, III, 176.

[99] Johnson, *Lives,* I, 401.

[100] Quoted thirty-seven times under E and F.

[101] *Harleian Catalogue,* I, 487.

[102] Johnson quotes Chapman nineteen times under A, B, C—one hundred five
times under Q, R, S.

[103] Quotations under *bright, stretcher, strictly,* etc., added in the revised edition
of the *Dictionary.*

[104] Johnson, *Life of Dryden, Lives,* II, 110, 184; *Life of Pope, Lives,* IV,
39-40, 210.

Johnson's knowledge of Drayton[105] is even more striking. He knew the *Ode Written in the Peak*,[106] *An Amouret Anacreontic*,[107] the *Quest of Cynthia, Nymphidia,* and *Polyolbion,* the last three being especial favorites of his. For quotation in the *Dictionary* he used, as we should expect, the first complete edition of Drayton, which was published in 1748, with an introduction by his friend, William Oldys.[108] That Johnson should have been so fond of a poem about fairies is more unexpected than his devotion to Tusser. He quotes from *Nymphidia* again some years later to point out the parallel between Drayton's Puck and Shakespeare's;[109] and he shows his familiarity with *Polyolbion* in his notes on *King John* and *Henry VIII*,[110] and again in the *Life of Dryden.*[111]

With some of the lesser Jacobean poets he had at least a passing acquaintance. He knew Wotton, both his prose and verse,[112] and Sir Joseph Beaumont slightly. Aleyn and Taylor the Water Poet he knew better. Knowing that Johnson had made a thorough survey of the works of Taylor,[113] we are not surprised to find him quoted in the *Dictionary.*[114] With Aleyn's poetical *History of Henry VII* he was familiar enough to discover a plagiarism of Prior's.[115] He had been reading the *History of Henry VII* about this time (1750-1752) while at work on the *Dictionary.*[116] Sir Joseph Beaumont's philosophical-theological

---

[105] Johnson quotes Drayton thirty-eight times under P, Q, R.

[106] Quoted in Johnson's treatment of Prosody, Introduction to *Dictionary.*

[107] *ibid.*

[108] See Appendix. A copy of this edition is Item 356, p. 17, in the *Catalogue* of Johnson's library.

[109] Johnson, *Shakespeare,* 1765, I, 104-5; 107, 134; also in notes on the *Tempest,* I, 69.

[110] *ibid.,* III, 413; V, 486.

[111] Johnson, *Lives,* II, 185.

[112] He quotes Wotton's verse under *belief, chanter, chastely, cheerer, cray,* etc. He also writes in his notes on *Love's Labours Lost, Shakespeare,* 1765, II, 173: 'Something like this is a stanza of Sir *Henry Wotton,* of which the poetical reader will forgive the insertion. . . .' He quotes the first stanza of *Ye Meaner Beauties of the Night.* Percy quotes this poem in the *Reliques,* I, 280-1, but gives a different version; and Percy was unaware that it was written by Sir Henry Wotton.

[113] Hawkins, *Life,* p. 141.

[114] Only under *accidence* (in first edition).

[115] Johnson, *Rambler No. 143, Works,* VI, 20-1.

[116] He quotes Aleyn under *bow* (in first edition).

Psyche interested him sufficiently for him to quote from it occasionally, most of the quotations being added in the revised edition.[117]

Of the numerous minor verse translators of this period Johnson knew Fairfax and May exceedingly well, and Sylvester, Holyday, George Sandys,[118] and Sherburne to some extent. In the sixty-ninth number of the *Idler*[119] he considers briefly the whole history of English translations, and though some important names are lacking, he is on easy and familiar ground. Translation is a subject which had long interested him, as we see especially in his lives of Dryden and Pope. He passes judgment with convincing self-confidence: '. . . the accuracy of *Jonson* found more imitators than the elegance of *Fairfax*; and *May, Sandys,* and *Holyday* confined themselves to the toil of rendering line for line, not indeed with equal felicity, for *May* and *Sandys* were poets, and *Holyday* only a scholar and a critick.'[120] Many years later Johnson has occasion to consider this group of poets again, in relation to Cowley and Dryden, and he does so with the same assurance.[121]

Johnson had only the slightest acquaintance with Sylvester's *Du Bartas,* the one bit of evidence being the quotation (under *periwig*) of the familiar lines:

'Now when the winter's keener breath began
To crystallize the Baltick ocean,
To glaze the lakes, to bridle up the floods,
And periwig with snow the bald-pate woods.'

He quotes from Sherburne, too, only once (under *interpreter*) in the *Dictionary*—and that not until the revised edition. But he

[117] Johnson quotes from Beaumont seven times in the *Dictionary*; of these the quotations under *aleberry, milk, stateliness, tactile,* and *won* were added in the revised *Dictionary*.

[118] Johnson discovered a copy of the 1636 edition of George Sandys' *A Paraphrase upon the Psalmes of David* in the library of the monastery at St. Cloud on his French tour, and, according to Boswell, read it there. See Tyson & Guppy, *French Journals of Mrs. Thrale and Dr. Johnson,* pp. 181-2, and notes 1 and 3, p. 182.

[119] Johnson, *Works,* VII, 275.

[120] *ibid.,* VII, 277.

[121] Johnson, *Lives,* I, 98 (May and Sandys); II, 118 (Sandys and Holyday); II, 158 (Stapylton and Holyday).

knew Sherburne better than Sylvester and speaks of his translations with praise: '*Sherbourn, whose learning was eminent, and who had no need of any excuse to pass slightly over obscurities, is the only writer who in later times has attempted to justify or revive the ancient severity.*'[122] Under the first four letters in the *Dictionary* he quotes May eleven, Sandys sixteen, and Fairfax forty-two times. He knew May's translation of Lucan's *Pharsalia* and Virgil's *Georgics,* Sandys' *Ovid*[123] and *Paraphrase of Job;* but best of all he knew Fairfax's version of the *Jerusalem.* Johnson at one time planned a new edition of Fairfax's *Tasso,* with notes and a glossary.[124]

IV

By far the two most important and influential poets of the first quarter of the seventeenth century were Jonson and Donne. They were born within one and died within six years of each other. Both were writing poetry before the death of Queen Elizabeth, but most of their work comes after; and owing to the fact that they together determined to a large extent the whole development of seventeenth century verse till the time of Dryden, it is more convenient to consider them in connection with the Metaphysical and Cavalier poets.

Johnson, as we have already seen, knew a few of Ben Jonson's plays well, but he did not know them all and never mentions the three greatest—the *Alchemist,* the *Silent Woman,* and *Volpone.* But if his knowledge of Jonson as a dramatist was deficient, there can be no doubt that he knew his poems and verse translations from the classics extremely well. He quotes in the *Dictionary* repeatedly from the *Fairy Prince,*[125] the *Tavern Academy,*[126] the *Epigrams,*[127] the *Gypsies,*[128] the *Owls,*[129] and from the collections of short lyrics, *Underwoods*[130] and the *Forest.*[131]

---

[122] Johnson, *Works,* VII, 278.
[123] A copy of the 1640 edition is Item 356, p. 17, in the *Catalogue* of Johnson's library.
[124] Boswell, *Life,* IV, 439. Also Hawkins, *Life,* p. 82.
[125] Under *agone.*
[126] Under *caterer, drawer, waiter.*   [128] Under *flirt, gill, knack.*
[127] Under *cony.*   [129] Under *flush, make.*
[130] Under *adjute, afeard, emissary, girth, nard, smutch, weft.*
[131] Under *court, gin, man.*
Note: These lists are, of course, far from complete. Numbers of the quotations

We do not usually think of Johnson as a lover of lyric poetry. Perhaps it is the thought of his own poems and a tendency to overemphasize his predilection for a more moral and philosophical type of poetry which is responsible; at any rate, to most of us it is far less surprising to discover his great admiration for the little known poem of Sir John Davies, *On the Immortality of the Soul,* than to find him deeply interested in Drayton's *Nymphidia* and the lyrics of Ben Jonson. Johnson enjoyed lyric poetry more than is commonly believed. He devoted one number of the *Rambler*[132] to the problem of criticism and lyric poetry; and his appreciation of the lyrics of Jonson and his sons is genuine if limited. It is curious that he seems not to have known Herrick at all.[133]

It is in the Cavalier poetry of the seventeenth century that Jonson's influence is most clearly traced. Despite the *Mistress,* Johnson is in the main right when he says: 'It is related by Clarendon, that Cowley always acknowledged his obligation to the learning and industry of Jonson; but I have found no traces of Jonson in his works: to emulate Donne, appears to have been his purpose.'[134] It is for this reason that he quotes so extensively from Donne in his *Life of Cowley.* He had no doubt about Cowley's debt to Donne and Donne's supreme importance in any consideration of metaphysical poetry. It is mistaken to believe that Johnson quotes from Donne in those famous passages only to heap ridicule on his poetry. It is true that he uses Donne to illustrate some of the extravagancies of metaphysical conceits; so he naturally takes extreme instances. That he quotes so extensively is one evidence of his familiarity with Donne's poetry. To deduce from the *Life of Cowley* that Johnson felt only ridicule for Donne would be to mistake his purpose in using those illustrations and do Johnson himself an injustice.

from Jonson have not been verified. For statistics on total quotations from Jonson, see note 31, p. 63, above.

Johnson also quotes Jonson in his *Life of Edmund Smith, Lives,* II, 225; *Shakespeare,* 1773, II, 32.

[132] Johnson, *Rambler No. 158, Works,* VI, 107.
[133] So far as I have been able to discover, Johnson never once mentions Herrick.
[134] Johnson, *Life of Cowley, Lives,* I, 89.

Johnson knew Donne's poetry thoroughly—how thoroughly one does not realize until searching through the *Dictionary,* where he quotes Donne steadily from the beginning to the end.[135] He quotes Donne more often than Ben Jonson, and he quotes from practically the whole range of Donne's poetry[136]—the *Songs and Sonets,* the *Elegies,* the *Epithalamions, Verse Letters, Satires,*

---

[135] For instance, ninety-seven times under Q, R, S.

[136] Johnson never gives the name of the poems of Donne's from which he quotes. A few will illustrate sufficiently the extent of his knowledge of Donne's work:

Songs and Sonets—
   *Valediction: Forbidding Mourning—*In the *Dictionary* under *compass, sublunary. Life of Cowley, Lives,* I, 52-3.
   *The Canonization—*In the *Dictionary* under *litigious.*
   *Nocturnall upon S. Lucies Day—*under *hydropick.*
   *Loves Usury—*under *quelquechose.*
   *Valediction: Forbidding Weeping—*under *valediction.*
   *Go and Catch a Falling Star—*under *mandrake, snow.*
   *The Ecstacy—*under *sepulchral.*
   *The Funeral—*under *shroud.*
   Twicknam Garden—Life of Cowley, Lives, I, 49.
   Valediction: Of my Name in a Window—Lives, I, 41.
   Valediction: Of Weeping—Lives, I, 38.
Elegies—
   No. VIII. The Comparison—Lives, I, 49.
   *No. IX. The Autumnal—*under *autumnal, anachorite, antique.*
   *No. XIV. Tale of a Citizen—*under *sign.*
Epithalamions—
   On the Lady Elizabeth—Life of Cowley, Lives, I, 38.
   For Lord Somerset—ibid., I, 45.
Satires—
   *Satire I—*under *antique.*
   *Satire IV—*under *grogeram, sleeveless, tuftaffety.*
Verse Letters—
   *The Calm: to Mr. Christopher Brooke—*under *frippery.*
   First Letter to the Countess of Bedford—Lives, I, 34.
   *Second Letter to the Countess of Bedford—*under *ostracism.*
   Third Letter to the Countess of Bedford—Lives, I, 34.
   To Mr. R. W.—Lives, I, 35.
   To Mr. B. B.—ibid., I, 46-7.
   *To Mr. T. W.—*under *surquedry.*
Epicedes and Obsequies—
   *First Anniversary—*under *microcosm.*
   Second Anniversary—Lives, I, 47.
   *Elegie upon Prince Henry—*under *quotidian.*
   Obsequies to Lord Harrington—Lives, I, 39; I, 50-1.
   Elegie on L. C.—ibid., I, 44.
   *Elegie on Death—*under *sapphirine.*

and *Epicedes*. His quotations are from the edition of 1719.[137] He does not seem to have cared for Donne's religious verse; his favorite poems, in fact, are altogether surprising. In his *Life of Pope* he speaks slightingly of the *Satires*,[138] yet he evidently knew them well[139] and quoted from them freely. It is even more surprising to find him quoting, not in the *Life of Cowley* as an example of extravagance, but in the *Dictionary* from the most extreme of Donne's *Elegies*—the one on Prince Henry; and from the Fourteenth Elegy, *Tale of a Citizen,* the lines:

'I found my miss, struck hands, and made him tell,
To hold acquaintance still, where he did dwell;
He barely nam'd the street, promis'd the wine,
But his wife gave me the very sign.'

But most surprising of all is his partiality for Donne's love poems and early songs. Special favorites of his seem to have been the *Autumnal*, the *Valediction Forbidding Mourning,* which he liked for its ingenuity, and the song *Go and Catch a Falling Star*. This song and the *Funeral* he even knew well enough to quote (or misquote) from memory.[140]

Johnson's criticism of the Metaphysical School is not altogether adverse. He accepted the standard of poetry laid down by Dryden and Pope, which means that he expected smoothness of verse, careful modulation, elegance of diction, naturalness of wit. Naturally, judging by these criteria, he was bound to censure the metaphysical poets. He objected on principle to their far-

---

[137] See Appendix.
[138] Johnson, *Lives*, IV, 116.
[139] Besides the *Dictionary*, Johnson refers to Donne's *Satires* in his *Shakespeare*, 1765, II, 55.
[140] Johnson, under *shroud*, gives, incorrectly and missing out a verse:
'Whoever comes to shroud me, do not harm
That subtle wreath of hair about my arm.'

Under *snow* he quotes:
'If thou be'st born to see strange sights,
Ride ten thousand days and nights
Till age snow white hairs on thee.'

The correct lines in the edition he used are:
'If thou be'st born to strange sights,
Things invisible go see,
Ride ten thousand dayes and nights,
Till age snow white hairs on thee.'

fetched conceits, though he could not help occasionally admiring their ingenuity. He was troubled by what seemed to him the unwarranted harshness of their versification, their way of drawing their pains 'through rhyme's vexation.' It is this lack of smoothness and modulation which made him say that 'instead of writing poetry, they only wrote verses.' He was less severe than Ben Jonson.

Despite his natural and inherited bias against their method of writing poetry, Johnson could not help admiring the Metaphysicals in many respects. Like Dryden, he allowed them to be wits. He knew that 'they sometimes struck out unexpected truth,' that 'their conceits were often worth the carriage.' Above all, with his confirmed dislike of imitative poetry, he appreciated and admired their originality, their native vigor. It is true that he placed Cowley above Donne, as 'undoubtedly the best' poet of the group,[141] but his reason for so doing was only that Cowley's versification was less rugged than Donne's. In the passage on metaphysical poetry, it is Cowley's aberrations that he ridicules most, not Donne's; and of the fourteen times he quotes from Donne in that passage, in five instances it is with qualified praise. It is no mean tribute to Donne that Johnson, despite his different conception of poetry, felt such a keen interest in his work.

The poet who, of all the Metaphysicals, was the most extreme in his conceits was John Cleveland. In his *Life of Cowley* Johnson cites two of Cleveland's extravagances, and he could have cited more if he had wished, for he knew Cleveland's poetry well. When he wrote the *Life of Cowley* he had been reading Cleveland for twenty-five years. In the first edition of the *Dictionary* he quotes with relative frequency from Cleveland, and he adds a few more quotations in the edition of 1773.[142] In his *Life of Parnell* he writes: 'The hint of the *Hymn to Contentment* I suspect to have been borrowed from Cleiveland.'[143] And he did not read Cleveland only to be amused by extravagancies, for his

---

[141] The quotations in this and the preceding paragraph are from the *Life of Cowley*.

[142] Johnson does not quote from Cleveland under A and B; but he quotes from him fifteen times under C, D, E. The quotations under *concorporate* and *confection* do not appear in the first edition.

[143] Johnson, *Lives*, II, 290.

quotations in the *Dictionary* show clearly that he appreciated Cleveland's lucid intervals. He believed with Dryden: 'Si sic omnia dixisset.' A *Life of Cleveland* by Johnson would have been among the most interesting of the biographies of minor poets he might have written.

Of the religious poets who were also metaphysical, Johnson knew Herbert and Crashaw,[144] and had a slight acquaintance with Quarles.[145] Like Pope, he was an admirer of Crashaw, preferring his poetry, in spite of its Catholic inspiration, to that of the Anglican Herbert; he was perfectly aware, too, that Pope at times copied Crashaw.[146] It is curious that he should have known the *Temple* and *Steps to the Temple* and yet seemingly have cared so little for Donne's religious poems.

Johnson's knowledge of the Cavalier poets varied. He had only a slight acquaintance with Randolph and Lovelace; he knew Carew somewhat better; and Suckling he knew better still. He quotes them all, except Lovelace, in the first edition of the *Dictionary*. He refers once to Lovelace in his notes on the *Comedy of Errors*,[147] and includes a quotation from him in the revised edition of the *Dictionary*.[148] From Randolph he quotes twice.[149] He had evidently been reading Carew between 1755 and 1773, for to the seven quotations from Carew in the first edition he adds twenty-eight more in 1773.[150] But Suckling he knew first and liked best; he quotes from Suckling, not very frequently, but steadily throughout the first edition of the *Dictionary*,[151] particularly from the *Ballad on a Wedding*.[152] He points out the possible

---

[144] He quotes from both steadily throughout the *Dictionary*. Under M, N, O—five times from Herbert; twenty-two times from Crashaw.

[145] He quotes from Quarles only once, under *cloth,* and then not in the first but in the revised edition of the *Dictionary*.

[146] Johnson, *Rambler No. 143, Works*, VI, 19-20.

[147] Johnson, *Shakespeare*, 1765, III, 125.

[148] Under *for*.

[149] Under *fulminate* and *worship*, the former added in 1773.

[150] Quoted under: *fair* (in first), *fire, fireside* (in first), *fishful, fresh, friend, frozen, light, meshy* (in first), *mistrustless* (in first), *more, mortality, mould, never, none, pine, pitcher, reave* (in first), *rogue* (in first), *sea* (in first), *shower, stamp, stow, sup, sweet, taste, uncreate, urn, wax, weave, win, with, within. worship, wrap*.

[151] Sixteen times under A, B, C.

[152] Under *carouse, Catherine pear, chaplets, glance,* etc.

source of one of Suckling's poems,[153] and of the whole group it is only on Suckling that he ever passes any critical judgment.[154]

Though not, strictly speaking, a Cavalier poet, Richard Corbet was a contemporary of the Cavaliers and wrote a small body of verse in a similar vein. Johnson never mentions Corbet except in the *Dictionary*. There he quotes from Corbet, not so much as from Suckling, but, like Suckling, in the first edition of 1755.[155]

Andrew Marvell survived the Restoration eighteen years and wrote the bulk of his verse—all of his satirical pieces—after 1660; but since the handful of poems for which he is most famous were written during the decade before, those poems come within the scope of this essay. Johnson knew Marvell[156] but seems not to have cared for his poetry. Whether on his own initiative he would have included Marvell in a more extensive edition of the English poets is doubtful.

With Marvell we come to the Restoration and to the limit of this investigation. None of the seventeenth century poets who appear in Johnson's *Lives* have, of course, been considered here. When we add them to the group of poets since Spenser whom he knew, but who were not included in the edition of the English poets, we begin to realize the extent of his knowledge of Elizabethan and seventeenth century poetry. And some of his favorite authors—Sir Thomas Browne, Jeremy Taylor, Robert Burton, Izaak Walton—do not come within the scheme of this essay. There can be no doubt that Johnson knew the literature of the seventeenth century and knew it well.

[153] Johnson, *Shakespeare*, 1773, III, 261.

[154] Johnson, *Life of Cowley, Lives*, I, 32, 57.

[155] He does not quote from Corbet, however, until the letter I—in all thirteen times.

[156] He quotes from Marvell only under *distrain*. Item 285, p. 15, in the *Catalogue* of his library is 'Andrew Marvell's works, by Thompson, 3 v. 1776.'

APPENDIX

Sources used by Dr. Johnson for the Dictionary[1]

I. ANGLO-SAXON

1. *The Anglo-Saxon Chronicle*:

   Chronicon Saxonicum. Ex MSS. Codicibus Nunc Primum integrum Edidit, ac Latinum Fecit Edmundus Gibson. A.B. è Collegio Reginae. Oxonii, E Theatro Sheldoniano A.D. MDCXCII.

   Johnson's quotation in the Introduction to the *Dictionary* (sig. d2ᵛ-e1ᵛ) is taken from the *Peterborough Chronicle* for the years 1137 (Johnson mistakenly gives 1135—in Gibson, MCXXXVII)-1140. In Gibson's edition this passage is to be found on pp. 238-44.

   A comparison of the beginning and end of this selection, and of salient points between, shows that Johnson is certainly quoting from Gibson's text. His quotation is identical with Gibson's version, save for one or two minor typographical errors.

   Note: Wheloc had previously printed the Parker MS., but that ends with the year 1070.

2. *The Boethius of Alfred*:

   An. Manl. Sever. Boethi Consolationis Philosophiae, Libri V, Anglo-Saxonice Redditi ab Alfredo, Inclyto Anglo-Saxonum Rege. Ad apographum Junianum expressos edidit Christophorus Rawlinson, è Collegio Reginae. Oxoniae, E Theatro Sheldoniano MDCXCVIII. Sumptibus Editoris, Typis Junianis.

   Johnson in the Introduction to the *Dictionary* (sig. c1ᵛ) quotes *Caput I, Caput II,* and the first paragraph of *Caput III*; in this edition, pp. 1-3.

   Johnson's quotation contains one or two slight misprints, but close comparison of the entire passage with Rawlinson's text leaves no doubt that this is the edition he used.

[1] References in this Appendix are to the sixth edition of the *Dictionary* (1785).

3. *Four Gospels*:

> *Quatuor D. N. Jesu Christi Euangeliorum Versiones*
> *perantiquae duae, Gothica scil. et Anglo-Saxonica.* . . .
> Thomas Mareschallus, Anglus: Dordrechti. Typis &
> sumptibus Junianis. CIƆIƆCLXV.

Johnson's quotation of the first chapter of Luke in his Introduction to the *Dictionary* (sig. c2ʳ-dlᵛ), eighty verses, was taken from Marshall's Anglo-Saxon text, pp. 169-78.

Johnson's version follows Marshall word for word, letter for letter, with only the slightest exceptions. Johnson's punctuation is identical—even including several full stops in the middle of sentences and the failure to begin some sentences with capitals. He omits the brief, bracketed parenthetical explanations which Marshall gives at the head of the chapter and between verses 25 and 26, 38 and 39, 55 and 56; but these are mere interpolations.

4. Hickes' *Thesaurus*:

> *Linguarum Vett. Septentrionalium Thesaurus Gram-*
> *matico-Criticus et Archaeologicus.* Auctore Georgio
> Hickesio, S. T. P. Oxoniae. E Theatro Sheldoniano.
> An. Dom. MDCCV.

(1) The first nine lines of Anglo-Saxon verse quoted by Johnson in his Introduction to the *Dictionary* (d2ʳ) are to be found in Hickes, Part I, 196. (Hickes quotes from *Bodleian, Digby* 4.)

(2) The rest of the Anglo-Saxon verses following the above nine lines immediately in the Introduction to the *Dictionary* (d2ʳ-d2ᵛ) are to be found in Hickes, Part I, 222-4. (Hickes quotes from *Bodleian Digby*, A.4.)

(3) Johnson's quotation in the Introduction: 'Fur in see bi west spaynge, etc.' (elᵛ) is to be found in Hickes, Part I, 231.

Johnson quotes the first two verses of this poem again under *cockney,* quoting also Hickes' footnote on the word, Part I, 231.

(4) In the Introduction Johnson quotes the first twenty lines from *Sancta Margareta* from Hickes, Part I, 224-5. Johnson's Introduction, sig. elᵛ.

Hickes mentions Robert of Gloucester in Part IV (*Dissertatio Epistolaris*), p. 27, and quotes thirty-three lines from the *Chronicle* on that page. These are not the lines quoted by Johnson. See Appendix XVI, *Robert of Gloucester*.

The Anglo-Saxon version of Luke, Chapter 1, quoted by Johnson (see Appendix I, 3) is not to be found in Hickes; though Hickes—Part II, 101-3—gives an Anglo-Saxon version of this same chapter, differing from the one Johnson found in Marshall's *Four Gospels*.

II. BALLADS

A Collection of Old Ballads, Corrected from the best and most Ancient Copies Extant. . . . London: MDCCXXVII.

Note: This is the only copy in the Bodleian. It is given in the *Catalogue* as a third edition; but only Volume I has on the title-page: Third Edition, 1727. Volume II has Second Edition, 1726; and Volume III, Second Edition, 1738. It is impossible to determine exactly which edition of this *Collection* Johnson knew. References in this work are to the Bodleian copy mentioned above.

1. Johnson in his *Shakespeare,* 1765, III, 183, has the note: '*Adam Bell* was a companion of *Robin Hood,* as may be seen in *Robin Hood's* Garland; in which, if I do not mistake, are these lines:

'"*For he brought* Adam Bell, Chim *of the* Clough,
   And William *of* Cloudeslea,
   To shoot with this forester for forty marks,
   And the forester beat them all three." '

In this *Collection,* I, 67:

'For he brought Adam Bell, and Clim of the Clugh,
   And William a Clowdel-le,
   To shoot with our Forester for Forty Mark;
   And the Forester beat them all Three.'

Johnson's version differs slightly, and he may be referring to another source; but he is quoting from memory, and when he does so is apt to be a little inaccurate. Percy in his *Reliques* has a ballad on Adam Bell, Clym of the Clough and William Cloudesly, but he does not print the stanza quoted by Johnson.

2. *Chevy Chase*:

(1) In this *Collection*, I, 111:

'To drive the Deer with Hound and Horn,
Earl Piercy took his way.'

Johnson, under *drive*:

'To drive the deer with hound and horn
Earl Percy took his way.'

(2) In this *Collection*, I, 114:

'At the first Flight of Arrows sent,
Full Threescore Scots they slew.'

Johnson, under *flight*:

'At the first flight of arrows sent,
Full Threescore Scots they slew.'

(3) In this *Collection*, I, 115:

'Like Lions mov'd, they laid on Load,
And made a cruel Fight.'

Johnson, under *load*:

'Like lion mov'd they laid on load,
And made a cruel fight.'

Percy, in *Reliques,* I, 240:

'Like lyons wood, they layd on load,
And made a cruell fight.'

3. *Johnny Armstrong's Last Goodnight*:

(1) In this *Collection*, I, 171:

'Is there ever a Man in all Scotland,
From the highest Estate to the lowest
Degree,'

Johnson (Boswell, *Life*, I, 466-7):

'Is there ever a man in all Scotland
From the highest estate to the lowest
degree,'

(2) In this *Collection,* I, 172:

'Yes there is a Man in Westmoreland,
And Johnny Armstrong they do him call,'

Johnson (Boswell, *Life,* I, 467):

'Yes, there is a man in Westmoreland,
And Johnny Armstrong they do him call.'

(3) In this *Collection,* I, 173:
> 'And run him through the fair Body.'

Johnson (Boswell, *Journal,* V, 48):
> 'And ran him through the fair body!'

4. *A Prince of England's Courtship to the King of France's Daughter*:
> In this *Collection,* I, 181:
>> 'In the Days of old,
>> When fair France did flourish,
>> Stories plainly told,
>> Lovers felt annoy.'

> Johnson, in his treatment of Prosody, Introduction to the *Dictionary*:
>> 'In the days of old,
>> Stories plainly told,
>> Lovers felt annoy.'

5. *The Children in the Wood*:
> In this *Collection,* I, 225:
>> 'No burial these pretty Babes
>> Of any Man receives,
>> Till Robin Red-breast painfully
>> Did cover them with Leaves.'

> Johnson, in the *Dictionary,* under *redbreast*:
>> 'No burial this pretty babe
>> Of any man receives,
>> But robin redbreast painfully
>> Did cover him with leaves.'

6. Ballad of *King Henry the IId*:
> In this *Collection,* I, 57:
>> 'A Cup of Lamb's wool they drank unto
>>   him then'

> Johnson, in the *Dictionary,* under *lambs-wool*:
>> 'A cup of lambs wool they drank to him
>>   there.
>>   *Song of the King and the Miller.*'

Note: The ballad *A Lamentable Song of the Death of King Leir and his Three Daughters* is in this *Collection,* II, 12-17; but the version differs slightly from that quoted by

Johnson in his notes on *King Lear* (Johnson, *Shakespeare,* 1765, VI, 160-3).

> For example: In this *Collection,* II, 14:
>> 'Forgetful of their promis'd Loves,
>> Full soon the same deny'd;'
> Johnson:
>> 'Forgetful of their promis'd loves,
>> Full soon the same denayd;'
> Percy:
>> 'Forgetful of their promis'd loves,
>> Full soon the same decay'd.'

This evidence, it will be seen, is not absolute proof that Johnson was quoting from this *Collection of Old Ballads,* attributed to Ambrose Philips; but when we take into consideration that in several of the above instances Johnson was quoting from memory, these slight differences seem of less significance. It is hard to believe that of the few ballads from which Johnson quotes six should by mere coincidence be included in the first volume of this *Collection.* That he had read at least this first volume seems highly probable.

III. BARCLAY

Stultifera Nauis, An. Do. 1570. . . . *The Ship of Fooles,* wherin is shewed the folly of all States. . . . Translated out of Latin into Englishe by Alexander Barclay Priest.

Colophon: Imprinted at London in Paules Churchyarde by Iohn Cavvood Printer to the Queenes Maiestie.

The selection quoted by Johnson in his Introduction to the *Dictionary* (sig. k4^r-k4^v)—'Of Mockers and Scorners, and False Accusers'—is to be found in this edition, fol. 80^v-82^r (in this edition leaves, not pages, are numbered).

A careful comparison of the first three stanzas and *L'Envoy* shows:

1. Johnson in line 1 has *Heartless* for *Heartles.*

2. Johnson in lines 11 and 12 has *wisdome* for *wisedome;* but in line 21 he has, correctly, *wisedome.*

3. Johnson has *c* for *C* in *Caytifs,* line 7 of *L'Envoy.*

Otherwise his text is identical with this, in spelling, punctuation, and so on. There can be no doubt that he used this edition. (The *Short Title Catalogue* shows no subsequent edition.) Also, at the end of this edition are printed 'Certayne Egloges of Alexander Barclay Priest.' See p. 50, above. Item 278, p. 14, the *Catalogue* of Johnson's library, is a copy of this edition.

IV. CAMDEN

Remains Concerning Britain : Written by William Camden. The Seventh Impression By the Industry and Care of John Philipot. London 1674.

Note : It is impossible to discover exactly which impression of this work Johnson used. A copy of Camden's *Britannia* is in the *Catalogue* of his library.

1. *Andrew Bourd* :

In this edition, pp. 23-4 : 'Doctor Bourd shall end these matters, who painted for an Englishman, a proper fellow naked, with a pair of Tailor's shears in one hand and a piece of cloth on his arm, with these rhimes : how truly and aptly I refer to each mans particular consideration :

> 'I am an Englishman, and naked I stand here,
> Musing in my mind, what garment I shall wear ;
> For now I will wear this, and now I will wear that,
> Now I will wear I cannot tell what :
> All new fashions be pleasant to me,
> I will have them whether I thrive or thee :
> Now I am a frisker, all men on me look,
> What should I do but set Cock on the hoop ?
> What do I care, if all the world me fail,
> I will have a garment reach to my tail ;' etc.

Johnson, in the *Dictionary,* under *sit* :

> 'All new fashions be pleasant to me,
> I will have them whether I thrive or thee ;
> Now I am a frisker, all men on me look,
> What should I do but sit cock on the hoop ?
> What do I care if all the world me fail,
> I will have a garment reach to my tail. *Bourd.'*

Johnson, in the *Dictionary,* under *cock on the hoop* :

> 'Now I am a frisker, all men on me look ;
> What should I do but set cock on the hoop ?
> *Camden's Remains.'*

2. In this edition, p. 522 : 'A Gentleman falling off his Horse, brake his neck, which suddain hap gave occasion of

much speech of his former life, and some in this judging
World, judged the worst. In which respect a good Friend
made this good Epitaph, remembring that of Saint Augus-
tine, *Misericordia Domini inter pontem, et fontem.*

> 'My friend judge not me,
> Thou seest I judge not thee:
> Betwixt the stirrop and the ground,
> Mercy I askt, mercy I found.'

Johnson (Boswell, *Life,* IV, 245): 'There is in *Camden's
Remains,* an epitaph upon a very wicked man, who was
killed by a fall from his horse, in which he is supposed to
say,

> "Between the stirrup and the ground,
> I mercy ask'd, I mercy found." '

Johnson quotes the *Remains* frequently in the *Dictionary*
and elsewhere in his works.

V. Chaucer

The Works of Geoffrey Chaucer Compared with the For-
mer Editions, and many valuable Mss. By John Urry,
Student of Christ-Church, Oxon. Deceased. London,
Printed for Bernard Lintot MDCCXXI.

1. Johnson in his Introduction to the *Dictionary* quotes
(sig. f2^v-g1^v) from the beginning of Chaucer's *Boethius.*
This passage is printed in Urry's edition, p. 359.

The first twenty-five lines in Johnson are identical with
those in Urry (word for word, spelling, punctuation), except for one slight variation in line 16:

Johnson: '. . . that he ne cometh not in yeres.'
Urry: '. . . that ne commeth not in yeres.'

2. Johnson in the Introduction to the *Dictionary* (sig.
g2^r): 'The conclusions of the *Astrolabie.* This book (written to his son in the year of our Lord 1391, and in the 14
of King Richard II.) standeth so good at this day, especially
for the horizon of Oxford, as in the opinion of the learned
it cannot be amended, says an Edit. of Chaucer.'

He then quotes seventy-two lines.

Urry's edition, p. 439: '*The Conclusions of the Astrolabie.* This Book (written to his Son in the Year of our
Lord 1391, and in the 14 of King Richard II.) standeth so

good at this Day, especially for the Horizon of Oxford, as in the Opinion of the Learned it cannot be amended, says the last Edit. of Chaucer.'

The first paragraph (thirty-five lines) in Johnson is identical with the same passage in Urry, except that Johnson occasionally reduces capitals to small letters in the middle of sentences.

3. Johnson's quotation from the *Prologue to the Testament of Love* in the Introduction (sig. g2^r-hl^r) is to be found in Urry's edition, p. 478.

The first paragraphs in both are identical.

4. Johnson's quotation from the *Prologue to the Canterbury Tales* (sig. hl^r) is the same as the text given in Urry, except for a few changes from capital to small letters; and in line 31 Johnson spaces *everych one,* whereas Urry's edition prints *everychone.*

5. The first ten lines of Johnson's quotation from the *Hous of Fame* (sig. hl^r-hl^v) are identical with the version in Urry, pp. 459-60.

6. Johnson's quotation from the *Gode counsaile of Chaucer* (sig. h2^r) compares word for word, line for line with Urry's text—p. 548—except for one or two capitals.

7. The *Balade of the village without paintyng* (Johnson, Introduction, sig. h2^r; Urry, p. 548) is the same in both.

Note: The Works of Our Ancient, Learned, and Excellent English Poet, Jeffrey Chaucer: to which is adjoyn'd, The Story of the Siege of Thebes, By John Lidgate, Monk of Bury. London MDCLXXXVII.

Page 445: *The Conclusions of the Astrolabie.* 'This Book (written to his Son in the year of our Lord 1391, and in the 14th of King Richard 2.) standeth so good at this day, especially for the Horizon of Oxford, as in the opinion of the Learned, it cannot be amended.'

Compare with the quotations from Johnson and Urry given above, section 2. Johnson is clearly quoting from Urry, who in turn is quoting from this edition—Speght's Chaucer, reissued by J. H.

The text of this 1687 edition of Chaucer which Dryden probably used, differs radically from that quoted by Johnson. The spelling in this edition is considerably modernized. There can be no question that Johnson used Urry.

VI. COOPER

The Muses Library; Or, a Series of English Poetry, from the Saxons, to the Reign of King Chas. II. London MDCCXXXVII.

1. Pages 19-22: A selection from Gower's *Confessio Amantis*. Not the selection quoted by Johnson in his Introduction.

2. Pages 24-9: Mrs. Cooper quotes the *Pardoner's Prologue* as her selection from Chaucer. Johnson never quotes this.

3. Page 30: Mrs. Cooper quotes eight lines from Lydgate. Not those quoted by Johnson.

4. Pages 34-44: Mrs. Cooper quotes a long selection from Barclay's *Ship of Fools*. Not the lines quoted by Johnson.

5. Page 49: Mrs. Cooper quotes Skelton's *Prologue to the Bouge of Court*.

Johnson quotes the first thirty-five lines of this *Prologue* in his Introduction (k2ᵛ) with the same unusual spelling— *Autumpne, vyrgyne,* etc.—but in line 24 he has *heed* and *is* where she has *head* and *his*. In these two spellings, and in the whole of his quotation, Johnson follows closely the text of the 1736 Skelton (see Appendix, XVII). The resemblance to Mrs. Cooper's version is explained by the fact that she, too, was quoting from the 1736 Skelton, the edition Johnson used for this quotation; but she was quoting inaccurately and he was not.

6. Pages 57-8, 83-6: Mrs. Cooper gives three of the six poems from Tottel quoted by Johnson in the Introduction to the *Dictionary*.

7. Page 87: Mrs. Cooper quotes the same six lines from Andrew Bourd quoted by Johnson under *sit*. Mrs. Cooper:

> All new fashions be pleasant to mee,
> I will have them whether I thrive or thee:
> Now I am a frisker, all men on me looke,
> What should I do but set cocke on the hoope?
> What do I care, if all the world me faile,
> I will have a garment reach to my tale. . . .'

Compare with Johnson and Camden (Appendix IV, 1). Mrs. Cooper may have been quoting from Camden; Johnson undoubtedly was. Johnson quite clearly was not quoting from Mrs. Cooper.

8. Page 312: Mrs. Cooper quotes Sir John Harington's *Against a Foolish Satirist*:

> 'I Read that Satyre thou intitlest first,
> And laid aside the Rest, and over-past,
> And sware, I thought, that th'Author was
> accurst;
> That, that first Satyre had not been his last.'

Johnson in the *Dictionary* under *overpass*:

> 'I read the satire thou entitlest first,
> And laid aside the rest, and over-past,
> And swore, I thought the writer was accurst,
> That his first satire had not been his last.'

Note: This satire does not occur in the 1613 or the 1615 edition of Harington's satires. But it is Epigram No. 41 in the First Book in the 1633 edition—*The Most Elegant and Wittie Epigrams* of Sir Iohn Harington, Knight, Digested into foure Bookes. . . . London, Printed by George Miller, MDCXXXIII. In this edition (Pp2) the text is:

> 'I Read that Satyre thou intitlest first,
> And laid aside the rest, and over-past,
> And sware, I thought, that th'author was accurst,
> That that first Satyre had not been his last.'

Mrs. Cooper evidently used this edition of Harington. If Johnson used it, he must have been quoting from memory; otherwise he sticks fairly close to the text.

9. Pages 333-42: Mrs. Cooper quotes from Sir John Davies' *Nosce Teipsum,* quoting from the second edition (1714) of Tate's Davies. Johnson's quotations under *accident, accord, acknowledge* from Davies are none of them included in Mrs. Cooper's selection. See Appendix VII.

In the light of this evidence, it is safe to say that Johnson did not use Mrs. Cooper's *Muses Library* for any of his quotations in the *Dictionary*.

VII. Davies

The Original, Nature, and Immortality of the Soul. A Poem. . . . Written by Sir John Davies. . . . London 1697.

(The Dedication is to the Earl of Dorset. Preface, and Lines *Upon the Present Corrupted State of Poetry,* by Nahum Tate.)
The Original, Nature, and Immortality of the Soul. . . . Written by Sir John Davies. . . . The Third Edition. London 1715.

Note : This 1715 edition is an exact reprint of the edition of 1697 in a different format. The Bodleian copy has on the fly-leaf the note : 'This is only a portion of *Nosce Teipsum,* first printed in 1599. It is here called the third edition under the supposition that the above was the only edition previous to Tate's in 1697.' This note is in Rawlinson's handwriting, and is incorrect. The 1715 was the third edition of the 1697 (Tate's), the second edition having been published in 1714. There is no copy of the second edition in the Bodleian.

Johnson quotes frequently from Davies, using Tate's edition, but whether the one of 1697, 1714, or 1715, it is impossible to tell, as the second two (at least the 1715) are close reprints of the first. In the 1715 edition :

Johnson's quotation under *accident* is stanza 8, section III, p. 33.

Johnson's quotation under *acquaint* is stanza 25 of the Introduction, p. 7.

Johnson's quotation under *bar* is stanza 21, section VIII, p. 54.

In these three instances he follows closely the text of Tate.

VIII. DONNE

Poems, By J. D. with Elegies on the Authors Death. London 1633.
Poems, by J. D. With Elegies on the Authors Death. London 1635.
Poems, By J. D. With Elegies on the Authors Death. London, Printed by M. F. for John Marriot. . . . 1639.
Poems, By J. D. With Elegies on the Authors Death. London, Printed by M. F. for John Marriot. . . . 1649.
Poems, By J. D. with Elegies on the Authors Death. To which Is added divers Copies under his own hand never before in print. London, Printed for John Marriot. . . . 1650.

Poems, By J. D. with Elegies on the Authors Death. To which Is added divers Copies under his own hand never before in Print. London, Printed by J. Flesher. . . . 1654.
Poems, &c. By John Donne, late Dean of St. Pauls. With Elegies on the Authors Death. To which is added Divers Copies under his own hand, Never before Printed. In the Savoy, Printed by T. N. for Henry Herringman. 1669.
Poems on Several Occasions. Written by the Reverend John Donne, D.D. Late Dean of St. Paul's. With Elegies on the Author's Death. To this edition is added Some Account of the Life of the Author. London: Printed for J. Tonson. 1719. (There is no copy of the 1719 Donne in the Bodleian. Mr. C. H. Wilkinson kindly allowed me to consult his personal copy.)

1. Johnson, under *quelquechose*:

    'From country grass to comfitures of court,
      Or city's quelquechoses, let not report
        My mind transport.'

  1633: 'From country grasse, to comfitures of Court,
      Or cities quelque choses, let report
        My minde transport.'

  1635: 'From countrey grasse, to comfitures of Court,
      Or cities quelque choses, let not report
        My minde transport.'

  1639: Same as 1635, except *minde* without the *e*.

  1649, 1650, 1654: Same as 1635, except *quelque* spelled with capital.

  1669: 'From Country grass to comefitures of Court,
      Or Cities Quelque-choses, let report
        My mind transport.'

  1719: 'From Country grass to comefitures of Court,
      Or Citie's Quelque-choses, let not report
        My mind transport.'   *Loves Usury.*

2. Johnson, under *sublunary*:

    'Dull sublunary lovers! love,
     Whose soul is sense, cannot admit
     Of absence, 'cause it doth remove
     The thing which elemented it.'

  1633: 'Dull sublunary lovers love
     (Whose soule is sense) cannot admit

Absence, because it doth remove
Those things which elemented it.'
1635, 1639, 1649, 1650, 1654: Same as 1633.
1669: 'Dull sublunary lovers love
(Whose soul is sense) cannot admit
Of absence, cause it doth remove
The thing which elemented it.'
1719: 'Dull sublunary Lover's love
(Whose soul is sense) cannot admit
Of absence, 'cause it doth remove
The thing, which elemented it.'
A Valediction forbidding mourning.

3. Johnson, under *litigious*:

'Soldiers find wars, and lawyers find out still
Litigious men, who quarrels move.'
1633: 'Soldiers finde warres, and Lawyers finde out
still
Litigious men, which quarrels move,'
1635: 'Soldiers find warres, and Lawyers find out
still
Litigious men, which quarrels move,'
1639, 1649, 1650, 1654: Same as 1635.
1669: 'Souldiers find wars, and Lawyers finde out still
Litigious men, whom quarrels move,'
1719: Same as 1669, except *finde* without the *e*.
Canonization.

4. Johnson, under *hydropick*:

'The world's whole sap is sunk:
The general balm th'hydropick earth hath
drunk;
Whither, as to the bedsfeet, life is shrunk,
Dead and interr'd.'
1633: 'The worlds whole sap is sunke:
The generall balme th'hydroptique earth hath
drunk,
Whither, as to the beds-feet life is shrunke,
Dead and enterr'd;'
1635, 1639: Same as 1633, except for *general*.
1649, 1650, 1654: Same as 1633, except for *general*,
sunk and *shrunk*.
1669: Same as 1654, except for *balm*.

1719: 'The world's whole sap is sunk:
The general balm th'hydroptique earth hath
drunk,
Whither, as to the beds-feet, life is shrunk,
Dead and interr'd.'

A Nocturnall Upon S. Lucies day.

5. Johnson, under *snow*:

'If thou be'st born to see strange sights
Ride ten thousand days and nights,
Till age snow white hairs on thee.'

1633: 'If thou beest borne to strange sights,
Things invisible to see,
Ride ten thousand daies and nights,
Till age snow white haires on thee,'

1635, 1639: Same as 1633, except for *dayes*.

1649, 1650, 1654: Same as 1633, except for *dayes* and
be'st.

1669, 1719:

'If thou be'st born to strange sights,
Things invisible go see,
Ride ten thousand dayes and nights,
Till age snow white hairs on thee.' *Song.*

Johnson must have used one of these texts of Donne; but,
as the above evidence indicates, he did not in this instance
follow his usual practice of reproducing the text fairly
accurately. 1 and 5 prove virtually nothing so far as text
is concerned; but 2, 3, 4—especially 2—are significantly
close to the 1719 edition as opposed to the others, despite
minor variations. The 1719 edition was set up, with some
editing, from the 1669 text (see Grierson). Johnson was
most probably using the 1719 Donne, occasionally editing,
as in 2 and 3, and modernizing the spelling. 5 looks suspiciously like a quotation from memory (which would be
extremely interesting), though it may, of course, have been
garbled by an amanuensis or the typesetter.

No copy of Donne is given in the *Catalogue* of Johnson's
library.

IX. DRAYTON

Poems By Michael Drayton Esquire. London 1613.
Poems: By Michael Drayton, Esquire. London N. D.
[1619].

Poems by Michael Drayton Esquyer   London. (No date on title-page; but on a second title-page opposite p. 158: *Englands Heroicall Epistles* by Michael Drayton, Esquire. London 1630. Opposite p. 496 there is a third title-page: *The Battaile of Agincourt* London 1631.)

Poems by Michael Drayton Esquyer. Collected into one Volume   London 1637.

The Works of Michael Drayton, Esq. Being all the Writings of that Celebrated Author, Now first collected into One Volume. London 1748. (Introduction by Wm. Oldys—unsigned.)

Note: The *Nymphidia* and the *Quest of Cynthia* are not included in the editions of 1613, [1619], 1637. Therefore, Johnson must have used another edition, either that of 1630-1631, or that of 1748.

Johnson, under *brier*:
'Then thrice under a brier doth creep,
Which at both ends was rooted deep,
And over it three times doth leap;
    Her magick much availing.
         Nymph.'

1748 edition (p. 165)	*1630-1631 edition (p. 182)*
'Then thrice under a brier doth creep,	'Then thrice under a Bryer doth creepe,
Which at both ends was rooted deep,	Which at both ends was rooted deepe,
And over it three times she leapt,	And ouer it three times shee leepe;
Her magick much availing:'	Her Magicke much auayling:'

Johnson, under *curvet*:
'Himself he on an earwig set,
Yet scarce he on his back could get,
So oft and high he did curvet,
    Ere he himself could settle.
         Nymph.'

1748 edition (p. 166)	*1630-1631 edition (p. 186)*
'Himself he on an earwig set,	'Himselfe he on an Earewig set,
Yet scarce he on his back could get,	Yet scarse he on his backe could get,
So oft and high he did curvet,	So oft and high he did curuet,
Ere he himself could settle:'	Ere he himselfe could settle;'

Johnson, under *span*:
'Together furiously they ran,
That to the ground came horse and man;
The blood out of their helmets span,
    So sharp were their encounters.
         Nymph.'

1748 edition (p. 167)	*1630-1631 edition (p. 190)*
'Together furiously they ran,	'Together furiously they ran,
That to the ground came horse and man;	That to the ground came horse and man,
The blood out of their helmets span,	The blood out of their Helmets ran,
So sharp were their encounters.'	So sharpe were their incounters:'

Johnson, under *consecrate*:
'Into these secret shades, cried she,
How dar'st thou be so bold
To enter, consecrate to me;
Or touch this hallow'd mold?
Drayton's Cynthia.'

1748 edition (p. 226)	*1630-1631 edition (p. 200)*
'Into these secret shades (quoth she)	'Into these secret shades (quoth she)
How dar'st thou be so bold	How dar'st thou be so bold,
To enter, consecrate to me,	To enter, consecrate to me;
Or touch this hallowed mold?'	Or touch this hallowed mold?'
The Quest of Cynthia.	*The Quest of Cynthia.*

Johnson, under *sleave*:
'I on a fountain light,
Whose brim with pinks was platted;
The banks with daffadillies dight
With grass like sleave was matted.'

1748 edition (p. 226)	*1630-1631 edition (p. 197)*
'At length I on a Fountain light,	'At length I on a Fountaine light,
Whose brim with pinks was platted;	whose brim with Pincks was platted;
The bank with daffadillies dight,	The Bank with Daffadillies dight,
With grass like sleave was matted:'	with grasse like Sleaue was matted.'

Since Johnson never follows the spelling of the 1630-1631 edition (and usually he reproduces faithfully the spelling of the edition from which he is quoting, as in the case of Chaucer, Skelton, etc.); since he is always nearer to the 1748 edition; and since in the third instance quoted above he cites the stanza under *span,* which is according to the text of the 1748 edition, whereas the 1630-1631 edition gives *ran,* it is certainly most probable that he used the 1748 edition of Drayton.

X. ELIZABETHAN DRAMA

The Works of Shakespeare in Eight Volumes with A Comment and Notes, Critical and Explanatory by Mr. Pope and Mr. Warburton. London. 1747.

The Plays of William Shakespeare. In Ten Volumes. . . . Notes by Samuel Johnson and George Steevens. London 1773.

1. 'Old Comedy':

Johnson, in the revised edition of the *Dictionary* (1773) under *rabato*:

'I think your other *rabato* were better. *Shakesp.*
'Broke broad jests upon her narrow heel,
Pok'd her *rabatos,* and survey'd her steel.
Old Comedy.'

Steevens' note on the line: 'Troth, I think, your other rabato were better'—*Much Ado About Nothing,* II, 288:

'Again, in the comedy of Law Tricks, &c. 1608:
' "Broke broad jests upon her narrow heel,
 Pok'd her *rabatos,* and survay'd her steel." '

2. Middleton:

Johnson, in the revised edition of the *Dictionary* (1773) under *poking-stick*:

'Your ruff must stand in print, and for that purpose get *poking sticks* with fair long handles, lest they scorch your hands. *Middleton's Blurt Master Constable, a Comedy,* 1602.

'Pins and *poking-sticks* of steel. *Shakespeare.*'

Steevens' note on the line: 'Pins and poking-sticks of steel'—*A Winter's Tale,* IV, 342:

'So in Middleton's Comedy of *Blurt Master Constable,* 1602:

' "Your ruff must stand in print, and for that purpose get *poking-sticks* with fair long handles, lest they scorch your hands." '

3. Beaumont and Fletcher:

(1) Johnson, in the first edition of the *Dictionary,* under *circle*:

'Has he given the lye
In *circle* or oblique, or semicircle,
Or direct parallel? You must challenge him.
                    Fletcher's Queen of Corinth.'

Warburton, in his notes on *As You Like It,* II, 380:

'This folly is touched upon with high humour by *Fletcher* in his *Queen* of *Corinth*:

' "*Has he familiarly*
Dislik'd your yellow starch, or said your doublet
Was not exactly frenchified?—
               —*or drawn your sword,*
Cry'd 'twas ill mounted? Has he given the lye
In circle *or* oblique *or* semicircle
Or direct parallel; *you must challenge him." '

(2) Johnson, in the first edition of the *Dictionary* under *starch*:

'Has he
Dislik'd your yellow *starch,* or said your doublet
Was not exactly Frenchified?
Fletcher's Queen of Corinth.'

Warburton, in his notes on *All's Well that Ends Well,* III, 91:

'So *Fletcher,* in his *Queen of* Corinth,
"*Has he familiarly*
Dislik'd your yellow starch, *or said your doublet*
Was not exactly frenchified?" '

Note: Johnson quotes both notes of Warburton's in his edition of *Shakespeare* (1765), II, 101; III, 376. Under *starch* he may have been quoting from memory.

(3) Johnson, in the first edition of the *Dictionary,* under *gord*:

'GORD. n. s. An instrument of gaming, as appears from *Beaumont* and *Fletcher. Warburton.*

' "Thy dry bones can reach at nothing now, but *gords* and *ninepins." Beaumont and Fletcher.*

' "Let vultures gripe thy guts; for *gords* and Fulham holds." *Shak.'*

Warburton, in his notes on the *Merry Wives of Windsor,* I, 265:

' "*Pist.* Let vultures gripe thy guts;[4] for gords and *Fulham* holds. . . ."

'[4] As for *Gourd,* or rather *Gord,* it was another instrument of gaming, as appears from *Beaumont* and *Fletcher's Scornful Lady—And thy dry bones can reach at nothing now, but* GORDS *or* nine-pins.'

XI. ELIZABETHAN NON-DRAMATIC POETRY

1. Shakespeare:

Sonnets: No quotations.
Venus and Adonis: No quotations.
The Rape of Lucrece: One quotation.

Johnson, in the first edition of the *Dictionary,* under *cloth*:

'3. The canvass on which pictures are delineated.

' "I answer you right painted *cloth,* from whence you have studied your questions." *Shakespeare.*

' "Who fears a sentence, or an old man's saw,
    Shall by a painted *cloth* be kept in awe."
                'Shakespeare's Tarquin and Lucrece.'

Warburton, in his note on the line, 'But I answer you right painted cloth, from whence you have studied your questions' (*As You Like It,* II, 341), quotes Theobald's note:

'This alludes to the fashion, in old painted hangings, of motto's and moral sentences from the mouths of the figures. The poet again hints at these in his poem, call'd *Tarquin* and *Lucrece:*

' *"Who fears a sentence, or an old man's saw,*
    Shall by a painted cloth *be kept in awe." '*

Note: Johnson also quotes this note in his *Shakespeare,* II, 59.

2. Marlowe—Raleigh:

Johnson, in his notes on the *Merry Wives of Windsor—Shakespeare,* II, 498-9:

'This is part of a beautiful little poem of the author's, which poem, and the answer to it, the reader will not be displeased to find here.'

Johnson, in the first edition of the *Dictionary,* under *youth:*

'But could youth last, and love still breed,
    Had joys no date, and age no need:
    Then these delights my mind might move,
    To live with thee, and be thy love. *Shakespeare.'*

Variations in the text of the two poems as given by Johnson in the *Dictionary* and *Shakespeare,* by Warburton, and by Percy:

Johnson (*field*):

'Live with me, and be my love,
    And we will all the pleasures prove,'

Warburton:

'Live with me, and be my Love,
    And we will all the Pleasure prove,'

Johnson (*Shake*. II, 498):
> 'Come live with me, and be my Love,
> And we will all the Pleasure prove.'

Johnson (*fold*):
> 'Time drives the flocks from field to fold'

Warburton:
> 'Time drives the Flocks from Field to Fold'

Johnson (*Shake.*):
> 'But Time drives Flocks from Field to Fold'

Johnson (*kirtle*):
> 'Thy cap, thy kirtle and thy posies'

Warburton:
> 'Thy Cap, thy Girdle, and thy Posies:'

Johnson (*Shake.*):
> 'Thy Cap, thy Kirtle, and thy Posies:'

Johnson (*kirtle*):
> 'Soon break, soon wither, soon forgotten'

Warburton:
> 'Some break, some wither, some forgotten'

Johnson (*Shake.*):
> 'Soon break, soon wither, soon forgotten'

Johnson (*slipper*):
> 'Fair lined slippers for the cold'

Warburton:
> 'Fair lined Slippers for the cold'

Percy:
> 'Slippers lin'd choicely for the cold'

Johnson (*youth*):
> 'Had joys no date, and age no need;
> Then these delights my mind might move'

Warburton:
> 'Had Joys no date, and Age no need;
> Then these Delights my Mind might move,'

Percy:
> 'Had joys no date, nor age no need;
> Then those delights my mind might move'

These examples show the difficulty in determining from which version of these poems Johnson was quoting. He says himself that he knew several versions. Except for the one quotation under *kirtle*, it seems that in the *Dictionary* he was quoting from the version given by Warburton in his notes (making minor changes) ; and that in his *Shakespeare* he was quoting from the version printed in the *Gentlemen's Magazine,* 1739. Quite clearly, he never quotes from the version in Percy's *Reliques.*

XII. GOWER

Io. Gower de confessione Amantis. Imprinted at London in Flete-strete by Thomas Berthelette the. xii. daie of Marche. AN. MD. LIIII.

Johnson's quotation from Gower in the Introduction to the *Dictionary* (f2ᵛ) is to be found in this edition in the Pro-logue, fol. 3ᵛ.

The whole of Johnson's quotation (thirty lines) is identical with the text of this edition, a copy of which is in the sales *Catalogue* of his library (Item 583, p. 26).

XIII. HAYWARD

The British Muse, or, A Collection of Thoughts Moral, Natural, and Sublime, of our English Poets: Who flour-ished in the Sixteenth and Seventeenth Centuries. By Thomas Hayward. London M.DCC.XXXVIII. (Three volumes.)

The quotations in this miscellany are arranged, not by authors, not chronologically, but according to an alphabeti-cal system. For example:

'Abb. (abbeys) Shakespear, Daniel, Browne, etc.
Abs. (absence)
(abstinence)
Acc. (accident)
(acclamations),' etc.

Such a collection of quotations was ready made for use in a dictionary illustrated by quotations ; and Hayward's range is remarkable.

A check of the first five words in each volume of the *British Muse* (Vol. I—*abbey, absence, abstinence, accident, acclamations* ; Vol. II—*gaming, general, generosity, gentle-man, gifts* ; Vol. III—*pandar, parasite, pardon, parents, parting*) against Johnson's quotations under the same words in the first edition of the *Dictionary* shows that the quota-tions are never the same, except that under *parasite,* Hayward gives, among his illustrative selections, a long quotation from *Timon of Athens,* including three lines quoted under that word by Johnson. Johnson, however, was very familiar with *Timon*; this one instance of agreement is most probably accidental. It is safe to say that Johnson did not use Hayward's *British Muse* for quotations in the *Dictionary.*

XIV. Lydgate

The tragedies, gathered by Ihon Bochas. Translated into Englysh by Iohn Lidgate, Monke of Burye. Imprinted at London, by Iohn Wayland. N. D. (Malone has on the flyleaf of his copy in the Bodleian the note: 'Printed about 1540.' *Short Title Catalogue* gives 1535 (?). *Bodleian Catalogue* gives 1558.)

A Treatise excellent and compēdious, shewing and declaring, in maner of Tragedye, the falles of sondry most notable Princes . . . translated into our English and Uulgare tong, by Dan Iohn Lidgate Monke of Burye. In aedibus Richardi Tottelli. Cum priuilegio. (At end—Imprinted at London . . . 1554.)

In the Introduction to the *Dictionary* (h2ᵛ) Johnson quotes forty-two lines from the Prologue to the Third Book of Lydgate's *Fall of Princes.*

A comparison of his quotation with the text of Wayland's edition shows clearly that it was not the one he used.

A close comparison with the text of Tottel's edition shows that Johnson's quotation is identical, with the following slight exceptions:

1. In the sixth verse of the first stanza Johnson (or the printer) misprints *tight* for *right,* thus making nonsense of the line. Since in black letter there are two *r's,* one for the interior of a word, the other (almost identical with *t*) for the beginning of a word, this mistake is strong evidence for Johnson's having used this edition. Either he or the printer has simply mistaken initial *r* for *t*.

2. Johnson puts a full stop at the end of the second and fourth stanzas—omitted in Tottel.

3. Johnson expands the contractions: $\bar{n}$ to *nn*; $\overset{e}{e}$ to *en*; $\bar{u}$ to *un*; $\bar{o}$ to *on*; *&* to *and*.

4. In the 39th line Johnson reads *menace* for *manace.*

5. Johnson corrects the misprint, *drike,* in the 14th line, to *drinke.*

The *Prologue to the Third Book* is on fol. lxvii^v in Tottel's edition.

XV. MANDEVILLE

The Voiage and Travaile of Sir John Maundevile, Kt. . . . Now publish'd entire from an Original MS. in the Cotton Library. London: Printed for J. Woodman, and D. Lyon. 1725.

1. The first selection quoted by Johnson in the Introduction to the *Dictionary* (sig. fl^r-f2^r) is, in this edition, Chap. XVII, pp. 217-26.

2. The second selection from Mandeville quoted by Johnson in his Introduction (sig. f2^r) is to be found in this edition on pp. 382-4—Chap. XXXI.

The first twelve lines are the same, except for a few changes from capitals to small letters, and Johnson's correction of 'mamy Londes and manye Yles' to 'manye londes and manye yles.'

XVI. ROBERT OF GLOUCESTER

Robert of Gloucester's Chronicle. Transcrib'd, and now first publish'd, from a MS. in the Harleyan Library By Thomas Hearne, M.A. In two Volumes. Oxford, Printed at the Theater, M.DCC.XXIV.

The 202 lines from the *Chronicle* of Robert of Gloucester quoted by Johnson in the Introduction (e2^r-fl^v) are to be found in Hearne, Vol. I, 260-7. Johnson follows Hearne's text closely, even preserving the ẏ.

XVII. SKELTON

Pithy Pleasaunt and Profitable Workes of Maister Skelton, Poete Laureate to King Henry the VIIIth. London: Printed for C. Davis in Pater-noster Row. MDCCXXXVI.

Johnson in his Introduction (k2^v) quotes the first thirty-five lines from the Prologue to the *Bouge of Court.* His quotation is identical (unusual spelling, punctuation, etc.) with the text of this edition (pp. 59-60).

Line 24 of the *Prologue* in Johnson, Mrs. Cooper, and the 1736 edition:

Mrs. Cooper:

'His head maye be harde, but feble, his brayne:'

Johnson:

'His heed maye be harde, but feble is brayne'

1736 edition:

'His heed maye be harde, but feble is brayne'

Johnson follows exactly the punctuation of the 1736 edition, whereas that of Mrs. Cooper is different. It is certain that both Johnson and Mrs. Cooper were quoting from this edition of Skelton, and that Johnson was not quoting from Mrs. Cooper.

XVIII. TOTTEL

Poems of Henry Howard, Earl of Surrey . . . with the Poems of Sir Thomas Wiat, and others his Famous Contemporaries. London: Printed for W. Meares at the Lamb, and J. Brown at the Black Swan without the Temple Bar. 1717.

1. Johnson's quotation in the Introduction to the *Dictionary* (k2ᵛ) of Surrey's *Descripcion of Spring, wherein eche thing renewes, save only the Lover* is printed on p. 3 of this edition. Johnson's version of the poem agrees, with the exception of a few capitals, with the text of this edition.

2. Johnson's quotation in the Introduction (k2ᵛ) of Surrey's *Descripcion of the restless estate of a Lover* follows the text of the 1717 Tottel closely. (In the 1717 edition, p. 3.)

3. Johnson's quotation in the Introduction (k3ʳ) of Surrey's *Descripcion of the fickle Affections, Pangs, and Sleightes of Love* compares exactly with the 1717 text (p. 4) for the first twenty-four lines.

4. Johnson's quotation in the Introduction (k3ʳ-k3ᵛ) of *A praise of his ladie* is to be found among the anonymous poems—in the 1717 edition, pp. 145-6. Johnson's quotation, the first twenty-eight lines of the poem, is identical with the text of this edition. This is the only one of the six poems he quotes from Tottel which he fails to quote in its entirety. In this edition the first twenty-eight lines are on p. 145, the second twenty-eight lines on p. 146. Johnson was probably in a hurry, neglected to turn the page, and quoted the twenty-eight lines on p. 145 under the impression that he was quoting the whole poem.

5. Johnson's quotation in the Introduction (k3ᵛ) of another anonymous poem, *The Lover refused of his love,*

embraceth vertue, in this edition is on p. 152. Johnson's version is exactly the same, except for a few capitals, and for line 12:

> Johnson: 'That is my honest desyre.'
> 1717 edition: 'That is my most desyre.'

6. Johnson in his Introduction (k3ᵛ-k4ʳ) quotes *The Death of Zoroas, an Egiptian Astronomer, in the first fight that Alexander had with the Persians*—in this edition, p. 258. Johnson follows the 1717 text closely, in the heading and the poem itself, except that in lines 4 and 5 he gives:

> 'Covered the ayre. Against full fatted bulles,
> As forceth kyndled yre the lyons keene,'

Whereas the 1717 edition reads:

> 'Covered the Ayre against full fatted Bulles
> As forceth kyndled Yre the Lyons keene,'

In spite of minor differences, the closeness with which Johnson follows the text of this edition, and the omission of half of poem 4, which is easily and naturally explained if he was using this edition, make it at least highly probable that Johnson was quoting in these six instances from the 1717 edition of Tottel's *Miscellany.*

XIX. WYCLIFF

The New Testament of our Lord and Saviour Jesus Christ Translated out of the Latin Vulgat by John Wiclif. . . . By John Lewis, A.M. London M,DCC,XXXI.

Johnson's quotation of Wycliff's version of the first chapter of Luke in the Introduction to the *Dictionary* (c2ʳ-d1ᵛ) is on pp. 35-6 of this edition.

Johnson follows the text of this edition closely, except that he divides into verses in order to make the parallel between Wycliff and the Anglo-Saxon version more clear. There are a few slight differences in punctuation.

———

> 'Tenants of the house,
> Thoughts of a dry brain in a dry season.'

SOURCES

Note: Editions given in full in the Appendix, unless frequently referred to in the body of the essay, are not given here. Works referred to only once are given, with the date of the edition, in the notes.

Boswell's Johnson, edited by George Birkbeck Hill, New York, 1891. (This edition in six volumes includes Boswell's *Life, Journal of a Tour to the Hebrides,* Volume V, and Johnson's *Welsh Journal,* Volume V.)

The Life of Samuel Johnson, LL.D., by Sir John Hawkins, Knt. London, 1787.

Letters of Samuel Johnson, LL.D., collected and edited by George Birkbeck Hill, New York, 1892. (Two volumes.)

Johnsonian Miscellanies, edited by George Birkbeck Hill, Oxford, 1897. (Two volumes.)

Anecdotes of Dr. Johnson, by Mrs. Piozzi, edited by S. C. Roberts, Cambridge, 1925.

The French Journals of Mrs. Thrale and Dr. Johnson, edited by Tyson and Guppy, Manchester University Press, 1932.

Dr. Johnson and Fanny Burney, by C. B. Tinker, New York, 1911.

Essay on the Life and Genius of Dr. Johnson, by Arthur Murphy. (See under Johnson's *Works,* given below.)

———

The Works of Samuel Johnson, A New Edition in Twelve Volumes, with an *Essay on His Life and Genius,* by Arthur Murphy, Esq. London, 1806.

The Lives of the Most Eminent English Poets; with Critical Observations on their Works. By Samuel Johnson. In Four Volumes. A New Edition, Corrected. London: MDCCLXXXIII. (Johnson's revised edition.)

The Plays of Wm. Shakespeare in Eight Volumes, with the Corrections and Illustrations of Various Commentators; to which are added Notes by Sam. Johnson. London, 1765.

The Plays of William Shakespeare. In Ten Volumes. . . . Notes by Samuel Johnson and George Steevens. London, 1773.

A Dictionary of the English Language, by Samuel Johnson, LL.D. London, 1755.

A Dictionary of the English Language, by Samuel Johnson, LL.D. London, 1785. (This is the sixth edition, but it reprints Johnson's advertisement to the fourth edition and is a reprint of that, the revised edition.)

A Catalogue of the Valuable Library of Books, of the late learned Samuel Johnson, Esq.; LL.D. Deceased; Which will be Sold by Auction (By order of the Executors) By Mr. Christie, At his Great Room in Pall Mall, on Wednesday, February 16, 1785, and three following days.

A Bibliography of Johnson, by W. P. Courtney, edited by D. Nichol Smith, Oxford, 1915.

***

The British Librarian London: Printed For Tho. Osborne MDCCXXXVII.

The British Muse Or a Collection of Thoughts Moral, Natural and Sublime of our English Poets Who flourished in the 16th and 17th Centuries. By Thomas Hayward. London, MDCCXXXVIII.

The British Theatre Containing the Lives of the English Dramatic Poets with an Account of all their Plays Together with the Lives of most of the Principal Actors as well as Poets. London, 1752. [Wm. Rufus Chetwood.]

Catalogus Bibliothecae Harleianae, In Locos cummunes distributus cum Indice Auctorum. Londini: Apud Thomam Osborne. Vols. I and II, MDCCXLIII; Vols. III and IV, MDCCXLIV; Vol. V, MDCCXLV.

A Catalogue of Books By Thomas Payne. London, 1801. [Catalogue of the library of Joseph and Thomas Warton.]

Essays, Biographical, Critical, and Historical, Illustrative of the Rambler, Adventurer, and Idler. . . . By Nathan Drake, M.D. 2 vols. London, 1809.

The Ever Green, Being a Collection of Scots Poems, Wrote by the Ingenious before 1600. Published by Allan Ramsay, Edinburgh, MDCCXXIV.

The Harleian Miscellany London Printed for Thomas Osborne. Vols. I and II, MDCCXLIV; Vols. III, IV, V, VI, MDCCXLV; Vols. VII and VIII, MDCCXLVI.

Johnson on Shakespeare, by Walter Raleigh, Oxford, 1929.

Linguarum Vett. Septentrionalium Thesaurus Grammatico-Criticus et Archaeologicus Auctore Georgio Hickesio, S.T.P. Oxoniae, E Theatro Sheldoniano, An. Dom. MDCCV.

A Literary Antiquary. Memoir of William Oldys, Esq. London, 1862.

The Lives of the Most Famous English Poets, or the Honour of Parnassus Written by William Winstanley, Author of the *English Worthies.* London, 1687.

The Muses Library Or a Series of English Poetry, from the Saxons, to the Reign of King Chas. II. London, MDCCXXXVII.

Northern Antiquities, Translated from Mons. Mallet's *Introduction à l'Histoire de Dannemarc,* etc. London, 1770.

Nugae Antiquae Being a Miscellaneous Collection of Original Papers in Prose and Verse. By Sir John Harington. London, MDCCLXIX.

Observations on the Faerie Queene of Spenser. By Thomas Warton. London, 1754.

Prolusions; or Select Pieces of Ancient Poetry. London, 1760.

Reliques of Ancient English Poetry. London. Printed for J. Dodsley in Pall-Mall, MDCCLXV.

Remains Concerning Britain Written by William Camden. The Seventh Impression. By the Industry and Care of John Philipot. London, 1674.

Shakespeare Illustrated, Mrs. Lennox. 1753-1754.

Shakespeare in the Eighteenth Century, by David Nichol Smith, Oxford, 1928.

Theatrum Poetarum, or a Compleat Collection of the Poets. By Edward Phillips. London, 1675.

The Union: or Select Scots and English Poems. Edinburgh, 1753.

Warton's History of English Poetry, by David Nichol Smith. Warton Lecture on English Poetry British Academy 1929. From the *Proceedings of the British Academy,* Volume XV. London, 1929.

The Works of Shakespear in Eight Volumes. . . . By Mr. Pope and Mr. Warburton. London, 1747.

INDEX

This index, with one or two exceptions, includes only authors and titles before 1660.

Account of a Servile Tutor, 73
Adam Scrivener, 40
Advancement of Learning, 59
Aeneid (Surrey), 53
Aeneis (Gavin Douglas), 47, 47n., 48n.
Against a Foolish Satirist, 95
Alchemist, 78
Alexander, William, 17n.
Aleyn, 7, 17n., 20, 23, 76, 76n.
All's Well that Ends Well, 103
Amoretti, 7, 66, 66n.
Amouret Anacreontic, 76
Anglo-Saxon Chronicle, 33, 85
Araignment of a Lover, 54n.
Arcadia, 7, 69
Armin, 17n.
Art of English Poetrie, 59
Art of Rhetoricke, 7, 56
Ascham, 6, 49, 49n., 56, 57
Astrophel and Stella, 7, 69
Autumnal, 80n., 81

Bacon, 7, 59, 59n., 60, 66
Balade of the village without paintyng, 93
Bale, 22
Ballad of King Henry IId, 89
Ballad of King Leir, 6, 46, 89-90
Ballad on a Wedding, 83
Ballads, 3, 6, 43-6, 87-90
Barclay, 6, 17n., 49, 50, 50n., 51, 52, 90-1, 94
Barnes, 73
Baron, 17n.
Battaile of Agincourt, 100
Beaumont and Fletcher, 5, 11, 62, 64-5, 64n., 65n., 102-3
Beaumont, Joseph, 7, 17n., 76, 77n.
Bedae historia ecclesiastica, 33n.
Beowulf, 33
Berners, 49n.
Bible (Wycliff), 33, 110
Blener Hasset, 17n.

Blurt Master Constable, 65, 102
Boethius of Alfred, 5, 32, 33, 85
Boethius of Chaucer, 40, 40n., 92
Boke of the Introduction of Knowledge, 51
Bottom the Weaver, 62n.
Bouge of Court, 51, 52, 94, 108-9
Bouncing Knight, 62n.
Bourd, 17n., 51, 52, 91, 94
Brandon, 17n.
Brefe Chronycle of Sir Iohan Oldcastle, 22
Britannia, 91
Brome, 17n.
Brooke, 20
Browne, 17n., 20, 106
Browne, Sir Thomas, 31, 84
Burton, 84

Caedmon, Ms., 33
Calm: to Mr. Christopher Brooke, 80n.
Cambyses, 60-1
Camden, 11, 42, 42n., 51, 51n., 59, 91-2, 94
Campion, 7, 17n., 73
Canonization, 80n., 98
Carew, 83
Catiline, 63, 63n.
Caxton, 9, 17, 37, 48, 48n.
Chalkhill, 17n.
Chapman, 7, 54, 55, 59, 65, 73, 74, 75, 75n.
Chapman's Homer, 7, 55, 75
Chaucer, 4, 5-6, 12, 16, 16n., 17, 17n., 28, 34, 36, 36n., 37, 38-42, 39n., 40n., 42n., 47, 48, 48n., 92-3, 94, 101
Cheke, 56
Chevy Chase, 3, 6n., 44, 44n., 45, 88
Children in the Wood, 6, 44, 89
Christ Kirk of the Green, 47n.
Chronicle of Robert of Gloucester, 33, 33n., 87, 108
Churchyard, 17n., 55

Civil Wars, 74
Cleveland, 82, 82n., 83
Coke's Tale of Gamelyn, 42
Collection of Old Ballads, 17, 45, 46, 46n., 87-90
Comedy of Errors, 75, 83
Comedy of Law Trickes, 65, 65n., 101 (*Old Comedy*)
Comparison, 80n.
Complaint of the Blacke Knight, 41
Complaint of Buckingham, 53
Complaint of Criseyde, 42
Compleat Angler, 71, 71n.
Confessio Amantis, 20, 36, 36n., 37, 37n., 94, 106
Constable, 73
Corbet, 7, 84, 84n.
Crashaw, 83, 83n.
Cuckowe and the Nightingale, 42
Cupid and Campaspe, 59n.

Dan Bartholomew, 54n.
Daniel, 7, 17, 17n., 59, 73, 74, 74n., 106
Davies, Sir John, 7, 17, 17n., 59, 73, 74-5, 74n., 79, 95-6
Death of Zoroas, 53, 110
Defence of Ireland, 75
Dekker, 17n., 61
Descripcion of the fickle Affections, 109
Descripcion of the restless estate of a Lover, 109
Descripcion of Spring, 109
Destruction of Troye, 48n.
Detection of Frauds and Tricks of Coney-Catchers, 59n.
Dioclesian, 64
Discourse of English Poetrie, 42, 59
Discoveries, 63n.
Doctor Faustus, 62
Donne, 7, 78, 79-82, 80n., 81n., 83, 96-9
Douglas, 17, 46, 47-8, 48n.
Drayton, 7, 8, 17, 49, 59, 73, 74, 76, 76n., 79, 99-101
Droome of Doomesday, 20, 54
Du Bartas (Sylvester), 77
Dunbar, 46, 47, 48, 51

Eclogues (Barclay), 6, 50, 50n., 91
Ecstacy, 80n.

Elegie on Death, 80n.
Elegie on L. C., 80n.
Elegie upon Prince Henry, 80n., 81
Elegies (Donne), 80, 80n., 81
Eliot, Sir Thomas, 49n.
Elizabethan Drama, 4-5, 5n., 19, 19n., 58, 60-6, 101-3
England's Heroicall Epistles, 100
Epicedes and Obsequies, 80n., 81
Epigrams (Jonson), 63n., 78
Epithalamion (Spenser), 66, 66n., 67
Epithalamion on the Lady Elizabeth, 80n.
Epithalamion for Lord Somerset, 80n.
Epithalamions (Donne), 80, 80n.
Essays (Bacon), 59
Ever Green, 45, 47
Every Island is a Prison, 45
Everyman, 60n.
Every Man in his Humour, 63, 63n.

Fabyan, 17n.
Faerie Queene, 66, 66n., 67, 68
Fairfax, 12, 17n., 77, 78
Fair Quarrel, 61
Fairy Prince, 78
Fall of Princes, 41, 42n., 107-8
Field, 61
First Anniversary, 80n.
First Letter to the Countess of Bedford, 80n.
Fisher, 6, 49, 50
Five Hundred Points of Good Husbandry, 55
Fletcher, Giles, 73
Fletcher, John, 64, 102-3; see also Beaumont and Fletcher
Fletcher, Phineas, 7, 68, 68n.
Floure of Courtesie, 41
Floure and the Leafe, 42, 43
Ford, 17n., 61, 65
Forest, 63n., 78
Fortescue, 48
Fortune, 40
Four Hymns, 66
Fruit of War, 54n.
Funeral, 80n., 81

Gardiner, 56
Gascoigne, 6, 17n., 20, 54, 54n., 55, 55n., 61

Glapthorne, 17n.
Glasse of Government, 54
Go and Catch a Falling Star, 80n., 81,
  99 *(Song)*
Gode Counsaile of Chaucer, 40, 93
Golden Garland, 46n.
Googe, 55
Gorboduc, 17, 53, 54, 54n., 60, 60n.
Governour, 49n.
Gower, 5, 17n., 20, 34, 36, 36n., 37, 41
  48, 94, 106
Grammar Construed, 59n.
Greene, 59, 59n., 61
Greville, 17n., 73
Grimald, 52, 53
Gypsies, 78

Habington, 17n.
Haddon, 56
Hall, 7, 17n., 59, 73, 73n., 74
Hamlet, 8
Harding, 17n.
Harington, 7, 17n., 20, 59, 73-4, 74n.,
  95
Hawes, 49, 49n., 51, 52
Henry IV—Part I, 60
Henry VIII, 76
Henryson, 46, 47, 47n., 51
Herbert, 83, 83n.
Hero and Leander, 75
Herrick, 7, 17n., 79, 79n.
Heywood, Jasper, 55
Heywood, John, 17n., 49, 61
Hick-Scorner, 60n.
Hieronymo, 60
Higgins, 17n.
History of Henry VII (Aleyn), 20,
  76
History of Henry VII (Bacon),
  59-60
History of Richard III, 50
Holinshed, 59
Holyday, 77, 77n.
Hooker, 7, 59, 59n.
Hous of Fame, 38 (Pope's *Temple of
  Fame*), 40, 93
Hundred Sundry Flowers, 54

Iliad (Chapman), 75
Induction, 53, 54, 54n.
Iohan Baptystes, 22

James I, 46
Jocasta, 54, 54n., 60n.
Johnny Armstrong, 6n., 44, 88-9
Jonson, 5, 5n., 7, 58, 62, 63-4, 77, 78-80,
  82

King, 17n.
King Alfred, 5, 30, 31, 32, 33, 33n.,
  37
King Alfred's Will, 30
King John, 76
King Lear, 46, 69, 90
King Richard III, 54
Kingis Quair, 47
Knight's Tale, 38 (*Palamon and
  Arcite*), 39, 41
Knolles, 7, 59, 59n.
Kyd, 17n., 60, 60n., 61

La Belle Dame Sans Merci, 42
Langland, 5, 17, 17n., 34, 35, 35n., 41
Latimer, 7, 56, 56n.
*Life and Death of Doctor Faustus,
  made into a Farce,* 62, 62n.
Life of Sir Thomas More, 6, 50
Lily, 17n., 59, 59n., 61
Linacer, 56
Lives (Walton), 71n.
Lodge, 17n., 59
Lovelace, 83
Lover refused of his love, 109-10
Love's Labours Lost, 76n.
Loves Usury, 80n., 97
Lucan's Pharsalia (May), 78
Lust's Dominion, 61
Lycidas, 4, 68
Lydgate, 5, 41, 41n., 42, 42n., 48, 94,
  107-8
Lyndsay, 17n., 46, 47, 48

Malory, 49, 49n.
Mandeville, 5, 32, 33, 34, 108
Marlowe, 7, 17n., 59, 61, 62, 62n., 71-2,
  104-6
Marston, 17n., 61
Marvell, 84, 84n.
Massinger, 17, 17n., 61, 65
May, 17n., 77, 77n., 78
Mead, 17n.
Measure for Measure, 72n.
Merry Devil of Edmonton, 61

Merry Wives of Windsor, 40, 70, 72, 103, 104
Mery Adventure of the Pardonere and Tapstere, 42
Middle English, 5, 28-37, 86-7
Middleton, 17n., 61, 65, 102
Milton, 2, 4, 8, 16, 19, 30n., 40, 42, 43, 53, 68
More, 6, 49, 50, 51
Morte d'Arthur, 49, 49n.
Most Elegant and Wittie Epigrams (Harington), 20, 74, 95
Mother Hubbard's Tale, 66, 66n., 67
Much Ado About Nothing, 102
Muipotmos, 66, 66n.
Musophilus, 74, 74n.
Myrrour for Magistrates, 20, 53, 54

Nashe, 17n.
New Inn, 63, 63n.
Nocturnall upon S. Lucies Day, 80n., 99
North, 59
Norton, 53
Nosce Teipsum, 7, 17, 74-5, 79 (*On the Immortality of the Soul*), 95-6
Notes of Instruction, 54
Nugae Antiquae, 13, 74
Nun's Priest's Tale, 39
Nymphidia, 7, 76, 79, 100
Nymph's Reply, 70-2, 72n., 104-6

Obsequies to Lord Harrington, 80n.
Occleve, 5, 17n., 41, 42, 42n.
Ode Written in the Peak, 76
Odyssey (Chapman), 75
Of Pride and of wast clothing of Lordis mene, 42
Of Singing Boys, 55
Old English, 5, 28-33, 85-7
Old English Gospels, 5, 30n., 33, 86, 87, 110
On Languages, and Particularly the Saxon Tongue, 31
Original, Nature, and Immortality of the Soul (*Nosce Teipsum*), 79, 95-6
Origins of the Drama, 60-1
Orlando Furioso (Harington), 20, 74
Orosius of Alfred, 33n.
Ovid (Sandys), 78
Owls, 78

Painter, 7, 56
Palace of Pleasure, 7, 56
Paraphrase of Job, 78
Paraphrase upon the Psalmes of David, 77n.
Pardoner's Prologue, 94
Passionate Pilgrim, 69
Passionate Shepherd, 62n., 70-2, 104-6
Pastorals (Browne), 20
Pearl, 33
Peele, 61
Peterborough Chronicle, 5, 32, 85
Phaer, 55
Philip Sparrow, 51n.
Physical Remains, 60
Piers Ploughman, 20, 34, 35
Piscatory Eclogues, 68
Pithy Pleasaunt and Profitable Workes of Maister Skelton, 108
Plays (Shirley), 20
Poems (Shirley), 20
Polyolbion, 7, 49, 76
Praise of his ladie, 53n., 109
Preston, 60, 61
Prince of England's Courtship of the King of France's Daughter, 6n., 89
Prologue to the Canterbury Tales, 40, 93
Prologue to the Story of Thebes, 41
Prologue to the Testament of Love, 93
Prothalamion, 66, 67
Psyche, 77
Puttenham, 59

Quarles, 83, 83n.
Queen of Corinth, 64, 102-3
Quest of Cynthia, 7, 76, 100, 101

Raleigh, 7, 17n., 59, 59n., 70-3, 104-6
Randolph, 17n., 83
Rape of Lucrece, 69, 70, 70n. (*Tarquin and Lucrece*), 103-4 (*Tarquin and Lucrece*)
Raston, 49
Reliques, 3, 6, 13, 17, 35, 35n., 45, 46, 46n., 47n., 49n., 54n., 59n., 60n., 71, 72, 76n., 87, 88, 106
Remains (Camden), 42, 42n., 51, 51n., 91-2
Restitution of Decayed Intelligence, 59

Robert of Gloucester, 5, 32, 33, 33n., 34, 37, 87, 108
Robin and Makyne, 47n.
Robin Hood, 6n., 46, 46n., 87
Roper, 6, 50
Rowley, 17n.

Sackville, 6, 17n., 53, 54, 54n., 61
Sancta Margareta, 34, 86
Sandys, 77, 77n., 78
Satire I (Donne), 80n.
Satire IV (Donne), 80n.
Satires (Donne), 80, 80n., 81, 81n.
Schoolmaster, 49, 49n., 56
Scornful Lady, 64, 103
Second Anniversary, 80n.
Second Letter to the Countess of Bedford, 80n.
Sejanus, 63
Shakespeare, 4, 5n., 6, 7, 8, 10, 11, 13, 16, 17n., 19, 38, 39, 44, 46, 49n., 50, 56, 57, 58, 58n., 60, 61, 62-3, 64, 65, 66, 66n., 69-72, 76, 103-4, 106
Shepherd's Calendar, 66, 66n. (Pastorals), 67, 68, 69
Sherburne, 77, 78
Ship of Fools, 6, 9, 50, 50n., 90, 94
Shirley, 17n., 20
Sidney, 6, 7, 17n., 39, 41, 58, 59, 67, 69, 73
Siege of Troy, 42n.
Silent Woman, 78
Sir David Lyndesay's Dream, 47
Sir Gawayne and the Green Knight, 33
Skelton, 1, 6, 17, 17n., 22, 49, 50, 51, 51n., 52, 94, 101, 108-9
Song of the King and the Miller, 6n., 89
Songs and Sonets, 80, 80n.
Sonnets (Milton), 4
Sonnets (Shakespeare), 7, 69-70, 103
Sonnets to Sundry Notes of Musicke, 69
Southwell, 73
Spanish Tragedy, 61; see Hieronymo
Spenser, 5n., 6, 7, 16, 17, 17n., 20, 41, 43, 48, 48n., 49n., 55, 58, 66-9, 84
Stapylton, 77n.
State of Ireland, 66n.
Steele Glasse, 54

Steps to the Temple, 83
Suckling, 83-4
Supposes, 54, 54n., 60n.
Surrey, 17n., 49, 52, 53, 53n., 109
Sylvester, 59, 77, 78
Syr John Froissart's Chronicle, 49n.

Take O Take Those Lips Away, 72n.
Tale of Beryn, 42
Tale of a Citizen, 80n., 81
Tamburlaine, 62
Tasso (Fairfax), 12, 78
Tavern Academy, 63n., 78
Taylor, Jeremy, 84
Taylor, the Water Poet, 7, 20, 76
Tears of the Muses, 66, 66n.
Tea Table Miscellany, 45
Tempest, 8, 76n.
Temple, 83
Testament of Criseyde, 42, 47, 47n.
Third Letter to the Countess of Bedford, 80n.
Thistle and the Rose, 47
Timber, 63
Timon of Athens, 107
To Mr. B. B., 80n.
To Mr. R. W., 80n.
To Mr. T. W., 80n.
Tottel's Miscellany, 6, 11, 17, 49, 52, 52n., 53, 53n., 94, 109 (Poems of Henry Howard, Earl of Surrey), 110
Tourneur, 17n., 61, 65
Toxophilus, 56
Travels (Mandeville), 33, 108
Treatise on the Astrolabe, 40, 92-3
Trevisa, 5, 9, 33, 34
Tunning of Elinour Rummin, 22, 52
Turberville, 17n., 55
Tusser, 7, 23, 55, 55n., 56, 76
Twicknam Garden, 80n.

Underwoods, 63n., 64, 78

Valediction: Forbidding Mourning, 80n., 81, 98
Valediction: Forbidding Weeping, 80n.
Valediction: Of my Name in a Window, 80n.
Venus and Adonis, 62n., 69-70, 103

Verse Letters, 80, 80n.
Verstegen, 59
Virgidemiarum, Satires in Six Books, 73
Virgil (Phaer), 55
Virgil's Georgics (May), 78
Volpone, 78

Walton, 71, 71n., 72n., 84
Warner, 17n.
Webbe, 41, 59

Webster, 17n., 61, 65
When flying Fame, 46n.
Whetstone, 55
Wilson, 7, 56
Winter's Tale, 102
Wisdom of the Ancients, 60
Wotton, 76, 76n.
Wyat, 17n., 49, 52, 53, 53n., 109
Wycliff, 5, 33, 34, 110

Ye Meaner Beauties of the Night, 76n.